SANTA BARBARA
TRAVEL GUIDE
2024

MIA AURORA

SANTA BARBARA TRAVEL GUIDE

2024

Discover The Charms Of Santa Barbara: A Coastal Oasis Blending Beauty, Culture, And Adventure.

BY

Mia Aurora

Copyright

Table Of Content

CHAPTER ONE

Introduction

1.1 My Last Holiday In Santa Barbara

Last summer, I embarked on a memorable holiday to the picturesque coastal city of Santa Barbara, a gem nestled along the sun-kissed shores of California. The trip was a perfect blend of relaxation, exploration, and cultural immersion, leaving an indelible mark on my travel experiences.

Santa Barbara welcomed me with its idyllic charm, boasting Spanish architecture, palm-lined streets, and a captivating Mediterranean climate. My accommodation, a quaint seaside cottage, provided a perfect retreat with its panoramic views of the Pacific Ocean. Waking up to the soothing sound of waves and the gentle caress of the ocean breeze became a daily ritual.

One of the highlights of my stay was the exploration of State Street, a bustling thoroughfare lined with boutique shops, charming cafes, and vibrant street performers. The vibrant atmosphere and the eclectic mix of shops ranging from high-end boutiques to local artisans created a delightful shopping experience. Exploring the boutiques, I discovered unique souvenirs, handmade crafts, and a variety of local delicacies that added a personal touch to my holiday.

Santa Barbara's natural beauty unfolded as I ventured to the Santa Ynez Mountains and the renowned Lotusland botanical garden. The mountains offered breathtaking hiking trails with panoramic views of the city and the Pacific Ocean. The Lotusland garden, on the other hand, showcased an impressive collection of rare and exotic plants, providing a tranquil escape into nature's wonders.

The city's commitment to art and culture was evident in its museums, and I spent an enriching day at the Santa Barbara Museum of Art. The museum housed a diverse collection, ranging from classical masterpieces to contemporary installations, offering a fascinating journey through art history. The vibrant art scene added depth to my understanding of the city's cultural fabric.

Culinary adventures were an integral part of my Santa Barbara experience. The city's seafood offerings, fresh from the Pacific, were a gastronomic delight. Sampling local delicacies at the Santa Barbara Public Market allowed me to savor the region's diverse flavors. From seafood tacos to artisanal cheeses, each bite was a culinary journey through California's rich food culture.

The evenings in Santa Barbara were magical, with vibrant sunsets casting a warm glow over the city. The Stearns Wharf, extending into the Pacific, became a favorite spot to witness the sun bidding farewell to the day. The wharf's restaurants offered a perfect setting for a romantic dinner, accompanied by the soothing sound of waves beneath.

My holiday in Santa Barbara was not only about leisure; it also included a touch of adventure with water activities. Kayaking along the coastline provided a unique perspective of the city, allowing me to appreciate its beauty from a different angle. The marine life, including playful dolphins and majestic pelicans, added a touch of wonder to the experience.

In conclusion, my last holiday in Santa Barbara was a harmonious blend of relaxation, cultural exploration, and natural wonders. The city's unique character, coupled with its breathtaking landscapes and vibrant culture, left an enduring imprint on my memory. Santa Barbara, with its Spanish flair and coastal allure, proved to be a haven of tranquility and a treasure trove of unforgettable experiences.

1.2 Best Reason To Visit

Santa Barbara is a charming coastal town located in California, known for its stunning beaches, Spanish colonial architecture, and laid-back atmosphere.

Beaches: Santa Barbara boasts some of the most beautiful beaches in California, with soft sand, clear waters, and stunning views of the Pacific Ocean. Popular beaches include East Beach, West Beach, and Leadbetter Beach.

Spanish Colonial Architecture: Santa Barbara's architecture is heavily influenced by its Spanish colonial heritage, with many buildings featuring red-tiled roofs, white stucco walls, and wrought-iron balconies. Notable examples include the Santa Barbara County Courthouse, the Presidio State Historic Park, and the Mission Santa Barbara.

Relaxed Atmosphere: Santa Barbara has a laid-back and relaxed atmosphere, making it a great place to escape the hustle and bustle of everyday life. Enjoy strolling along the beach, sipping coffee at a sidewalk cafe, or browsing the shops in the downtown area.

Wine Tasting: Santa Barbara is home to a number of wineries, offering a variety of wines to taste. Visit the Santa Ynez Valley, just north of Santa Barbara, to sample some of the region's best wines.

Outdoor Activities: Santa Barbara offers a variety of outdoor activities, including hiking, biking, kayaking, and surfing. There are also numerous parks and gardens to explore, such as the Santa Barbara Botanic Garden and the Mission Creek Park.

Arts and Culture: Santa Barbara has a thriving arts and culture scene, with numerous museums, theaters, and galleries. Visit the Santa Barbara Museum of Art, the Arlington Theatre, or the Faulkner Gallery to experience some of the city's cultural offerings.

Dining: Santa Barbara has a diverse culinary scene, with restaurants offering everything from fresh seafood to farm-to-table cuisine. There are also numerous cafes and bars to enjoy.

Events: Santa Barbara hosts a number of events throughout the year, including the Santa Barbara International Film Festival, the Summer Solstice Celebration, and the Old Spanish Days Fiesta.

Whether you're looking for a relaxing beach vacation, a cultural getaway, or an adventure in the outdoors, Santa Barbara has something to offer everyone.

1.3 Things To Avoid As a Tourist

Santa Barbara is a beautiful and charming city with a lot to offer visitors. However, like any place, there are a few things that tourists should avoid in order to have a safe and enjoyable experience.

Leaving Valuables Unattended: Santa Barbara is a generally safe city, but like any tourist destination, there is a risk of petty theft. To avoid having your belongings stolen, be sure to keep an eye on your valuables, especially in crowded areas like beaches and parks. Don't leave your bags unattended, and if you're carrying a purse or backpack, keep it close to you and zipped up.

Ignoring Parking Regulations: Santa Barbara has strict parking regulations, and it's important to be aware of them to avoid getting a ticket or even having your car towed. Pay attention to parking signs and meters, and don't park in restricted areas. If you're unsure about where to park, there are plenty of public parking garages and lots available.

Swimming at Unprotected Beaches: Santa Barbara has some beautiful beaches, but not all of them are safe for swimming. Some beaches have strong currents or rip tides, and it's important to be aware of the conditions before you go in the water. Only swim at beaches that are designated for swimming, and be sure to follow the instructions of lifeguards.

Hiking Without Proper Preparation: Santa Barbara is a great place to go hiking, but it's important to be prepared before you head out on the trails. Wear appropriate clothing and shoes, bring plenty of water and snacks, and let someone know where you're going and when you expect to be back. Be aware of wildlife, such as rattlesnakes, and don't feed or approach any animals.

Being Disrespectful of Local Culture: Santa Barbara is a diverse community with a rich history and culture. Be respectful of the local people and their customs. When visiting parks, museums, and other attractions, be sure to follow the rules and guidelines. Avoid making loud noises or littering, and dress appropriately for the occasion.

By following these simple tips, you can ensure that you have a safe and enjoyable time visiting Santa Barbara.

NOTE

_____

_____

_____

_____

CHAPTER TWO

Planning Your Trip

2.1 Best Time To Visit

Santa Barbara is a coastal city in California known for its beautiful beaches, Spanish colonial architecture, and laid-back atmosphere. The weather is mild year-round, with average temperatures ranging from the mid-60s to the mid-70s. However, there are certain times of year when Santa Barbara is especially pleasant to visit.

Spring (March-May)

Spring is a great time to visit Santa Barbara if you want to enjoy mild weather and fewer crowds. The average temperature in March is 65 degrees Fahrenheit, and the average temperature in May is 70 degrees Fahrenheit. The skies are usually clear, and there is little rain. This is also a great time to visit the Santa Barbara Botanic Garden, which is in full bloom.

Fall (September-November)

Fall is another great time to visit Santa Barbara, as the weather is still warm and sunny, but the crowds have died down. The average temperature in September is 75 degrees Fahrenheit, and the average temperature in November is 65 degrees Fahrenheit. The fall foliage is also beautiful in Santa Barbara, especially in the Santa Ynez Mountains.

Summer (June-August)

Summer is the most popular time to visit Santa Barbara, and for good reason. The weather is perfect for swimming, sunbathing, and surfing. The average temperature in June is 72 degrees Fahrenheit, and the average temperature in August is 75 degrees Fahrenheit. However, summer is also the busiest time of year in Santa Barbara, so expect higher prices and larger crowds.

Winter (December-February)

Winter is the least popular time to visit Santa Barbara, but it can also be a magical time to experience the city. The weather is mild, with average temperatures ranging from the mid-50s to the mid-60s. There is also less rain in winter than in other seasons. This is a great time to visit if you want to avoid the crowds and enjoy the city's peaceful atmosphere.

No matter when you decide to visit Santa Barbara, you're sure to have a great time. This beautiful city has something to offer everyone, from its stunning beaches and world-class wineries to its charming shops and delicious restaurants.

2.2 Weather And Climate

Santa Barbara, California, is known for its idyllic Mediterranean climate, characterized by warm, dry summers and mild, wet winters. The city's location along the Pacific Coast and its proximity to the Santa Ynez Mountains create a unique microclimate that sets it apart from other parts of California.

Summer

Summer in Santa Barbara is warm and sunny, with average temperatures ranging from the mid-60s to the mid-70s Fahrenheit. The humidity is low, making it feel comfortable even on the hottest days. Rainfall is rare during the summer months, with most of the year's precipitation occurring in the winter.

Fall

Fall in Santa Barbara is a transition season, with temperatures gradually cooling down from summer's warmth. The average temperature in September is 75 degrees Fahrenheit, and by November, it drops to 65 degrees Fahrenheit. Rainfall increases slightly in the fall, but it is still relatively dry compared to the winter months.

Winter

Winter in Santa Barbara is mild and wet, with average temperatures ranging from the mid-50s to the mid-60s Fahrenheit. Rainfall is significantly higher in the winter, with an average of around 5 inches falling between December and February. However, even during the winter months, Santa Barbara enjoys an average of 180 days of sunshine per year.

Spring

Spring in Santa Barbara is a delightful time of year, with temperatures steadily warming up from the mildness of winter. The average temperature in March is 65 degrees Fahrenheit, and by May, it reaches 70 degrees Fahrenheit. Rainfall decreases in the spring, and the city begins to transition back to its sunny, warm weather.

Overall, Santa Barbara's climate is a major factor in its appeal as a tourist destination. The city's pleasant year-round weather allows visitors to enjoy a variety of outdoor activities, from swimming and sunbathing in the summer to hiking and exploring in the milder months.

Here are some additional facts about Santa Barbara's weather and climate:

- The city averages around 36 inches of rainfall per year.

- The ocean temperature off the coast of Santa Barbara ranges from the mid-50s Fahrenheit in the winter to the mid-70s Fahrenheit in the summer.

- The Santa Ynez Mountains provide a scenic backdrop for Santa Barbara and help to moderate the city's climate.

Whether you're looking for a warm beach getaway, a mild winter escape, or simply a place to enjoy the outdoors year-round, Santa Barbara's weather and climate make it an ideal destination.

2.3 Packing Essentials

Packing for a trip to Santa Barbara, CA, can be a breeze with the right essentials. This charming coastal city offers a blend of relaxed beach vibes, Spanish colonial architecture, and a lively cultural scene. Whether you're planning a summer sun-soaked getaway or a cozy winter escape, Santa Barbara has something to offer everyone.

Clothing Essentials

Beachwear: Santa Barbara is known for its stunning beaches, so pack your swimsuit, cover-up, sunglasses, and a hat for protection from the sun. A quick-drying beach towel is also a must-have.

Casual Attire: Santa Barbara's laid-back atmosphere calls for comfortable and casual attire. Pack a selection of t-shirts, shorts, jeans, and skirts. A light sweater or jacket can be handy for cooler evenings or air-conditioned environments.

Footwear: Pack a pair of comfortable sandals for exploring the city's beaches, streets, and shops. If you plan on hiking or doing outdoor activities, pack a pair of sneakers for better traction.

Accessories: Elevate your outfits with a few stylish accessories like a scarf, hat, sunglasses, and a statement necklace. A versatile bag, such as a tote or cross-body style, can carry your essentials while complementing your look.

Toiletries and Essentials

Sunscreen: Protect your skin from the California sun with a broad-spectrum sunscreen with an SPF of 30 or higher.

Lip Balm: Keep your lips hydrated with a moisturizing lip balm, especially in the drier winter months.

Hand Sanitizer: Stay germ-free with a travel-sized hand sanitizer, especially when dining out or visiting public places.

Universal Adapter: If you're traveling from outside the US, pack a universal adapter to charge your electronic devices.

Travel-sized toiletries: Pack travel-sized versions of your essential toiletries, such as shampoo, conditioner, soap, and toothbrush.

Additional Tips

Check the weather forecast: Santa Barbara's weather can vary depending on the season. Check the forecast before packing to ensure you have the appropriate clothing.

Consider your activities: If you plan on doing any outdoor activities like hiking or biking, pack appropriate gear, such as a backpack, water bottle, and sunscreen.
Pack light: Avoid overpacking by choosing versatile pieces that can be mixed and matched. Roll your clothes instead of folding to save space in your luggage.

Bring a reusable water bottle: Stay hydrated and reduce waste by bringing a reusable water bottle to fill up at public water fountains or restaurants.

Leave room for souvenirs: Santa Barbara has many charming boutiques and shops, so leave some extra space in your luggage for souvenirs and goodies.

2.4 Language And Communication

Santa Barbara, nestled along the picturesque Californian coastline, is not only renowned for its stunning beaches and balmy weather but also harbors a vibrant and diverse linguistic landscape. As a hub for education, culture, and commerce, the city has attracted people from all corners of the globe, bringing with them a multitude of languages and dialects. This linguistic tapestry enriches the city's cultural fabric and fosters understanding and connection among its residents.

English, as the official language of the United States, holds a prominent position in Santa Barbara. However, the city's linguistic diversity extends far beyond this. Spanish, reflecting the region's historical ties to Mexico, is widely spoken, particularly in the city's vibrant Latino communities. Similarly, the influx of immigrants from Asia, particularly China, Korea, and the Philippines, has introduced a rich array of Asian languages to the city's linguistic repertoire.

The presence of the University of California, Santa Barbara (UCSB), a world-renowned institution of higher learning, further contributes to Santa Barbara's linguistic diversity. Students and faculty from around the globe bring their native tongues to the campus, creating a microcosm of the world's languages. This linguistic diversity is not confined to the classroom; it spills over into the surrounding community, enriching the city's cultural landscape.

Language is not merely a means of communication; it is also a vehicle for cultural expression. Santa Barbara's linguistic diversity manifests itself in a myriad of ways, from the multilingual signage that adorns the city's streets to the diverse array of international cuisines that tantalize taste buds. The city's cultural festivals and events provide a vibrant platform for showcasing the linguistic and cultural heritage of its diverse residents.

Santa Barbara's linguistic landscape is a testament to its rich history, its welcoming spirit, and its global connections. The city's embrace of linguistic diversity is a source of strength, fostering understanding, creativity, and innovation. As Santa Barbara continues to evolve, its linguistic landscape will undoubtedly continue to reflect the ever-changing tapestry of its people.

2.5 Currency And Money Matter

Santa Barbara, a coastal gem in California, boasts a thriving economy and a well-established financial infrastructure. The city's currency, like the rest of the United States, is the US dollar, with its familiar denominations of coins and bills. Banking services cater to the needs of individuals and businesses, offering a range of financial products and services. Santa Barbara's economy, a blend of tourism, education, and technology, fuels the city's financial vitality.

The US dollar serves as the official currency of Santa Barbara, seamlessly integrated into the national financial system. The dollar's stability and global recognition make it a reliable medium of exchange for everyday transactions and international commerce. Coins, ranging from the penny to the dollar, and bills, from the $1 to the $100, facilitate daily transactions, while larger denominations like the $500 and $1,000 are primarily used for large-scale transactions.

Santa Barbara's banking sector plays a crucial role in the city's financial well-being. Numerous banks, including national chains and local institutions, provide a wide range of financial services, catering to the needs of residents and businesses. These services include checking and savings accounts, loans, investment options, and wealth management services. The city's banking infrastructure ensures that individuals and businesses have access to the financial tools they need to thrive.

Santa Barbara's economy, a blend of diverse industries, fuels the city's financial vitality. Tourism, a major contributor, brings in visitors from around the world, boosting revenue for hotels, restaurants, and local businesses. Education, anchored by the University of California, Santa Barbara (UCSB), attracts students and researchers, generating economic activity and fostering innovation. The technology sector, with its presence of startups and established companies, contributes to the city's economic growth and dynamism.

Santa Barbara's financial landscape, characterized by a stable currency, a robust banking sector, and a diversified economy, provides a solid foundation for the city's continued prosperity. The city's financial strength supports its residents, businesses, and institutions, enabling them to pursue their goals and contribute to the vibrant tapestry of Santa Barbara's life.

2.6 4 Days In Santa Barbara

Escape the hustle and bustle of everyday life and immerse yourself in the charm and beauty of Santa Barbara, a coastal paradise nestled along the Californian Riviera. This 4-day itinerary is designed to help you experience the best of what this enchanting city has to offer, from its pristine beaches and historic landmarks to its vibrant culinary scene and world-class wineries.

Day 1: Arrival and Exploration

Morning: Begin your Santa Barbara adventure with a leisurely stroll along the picturesque Santa Barbara Harbor. Take in the panoramic views of the Pacific Ocean, spot playful dolphins frolicking in the waves, and admire the majestic yachts gracing the harbor.

Afternoon: Indulge in a delightful lunch at the Harbor View Cafe, savoring fresh seafood and enjoying stunning harbor views. Afterward, embark on a self-guided walking tour of the historic El Presidio de Santa Bárbara State Historic Park. Explore the adobe buildings, wander through serene gardens, and immerse yourself in the city's rich Spanish colonial heritage.

Evening: As the sun begins to set, head to the Santa Barbara Botanic Garden, an oasis of tranquility amidst the urban landscape. Stroll through the diverse gardens, filled with native plants and vibrant flowers, and discover the beauty of California's flora. Conclude your day with a delectable dinner at The Hungry Cat, where delectable seafood and innovative cocktails await.

Day 2: Beaches, Bliss, and Wine Tasting

Morning: Embrace the coastal lifestyle with a morning spent at East Beach, one of Santa Barbara's most popular beaches. Rent a surfboard or paddleboard and catch some waves, soak up the sun's warmth, or simply relax on the pristine sands and enjoy the ocean breeze.

Afternoon: Escape to the Santa Ynez Valley, renowned for its world-class wineries. Embark on a wine tasting tour, visiting renowned vineyards like Fess Parker Winery, Sanford Winery & Vineyards, and Firestone Vineyard. Savor the exquisite flavors of Santa Barbara County wines and learn about the region's rich winemaking heritage.

Evening: Immerse yourself in the vibrant arts scene of Santa Barbara. Visit the Santa Barbara Museum of Art, home to an impressive collection of paintings, sculptures, and decorative arts. Afterward, indulge in a delightful dinner at The Pearl, where innovative cuisine and a sophisticated atmosphere await.

Day 3: Hiking, History, and Culinary Delights

Morning: Embark on a scenic hike along the Jesusita Trail, offering breathtaking views of the Santa Ynez Mountains and the Pacific Ocean. Inhale the fresh air, appreciate the natural beauty, and capture memorable moments with panoramic vistas.

Afternoon: Delve into Santa Barbara's history at the Santa Barbara Museum of Natural History. Explore exhibits showcasing the region's diverse ecosystems, from marine life to dinosaur fossils, and gain a deeper understanding of the natural world.

Evening: Indulge in a culinary adventure at the Santa Barbara Public Market, a haven for foodies. Sample local produce, artisanal cheeses, and mouthwatering prepared foods, and savor the flavors of Santa Barbara's culinary scene. As the sun sets, enjoy a relaxing stroll along Stearns Wharf, lined with shops, restaurants, and lively entertainment.

Day 4: Coastal Charm and Farewell

Morning: Embark on a whale-watching excursion from Santa Barbara Harbor. Cruise along the picturesque coastline, spot majestic whales breaching the ocean's surface, and witness the wonders of marine life in their natural habitat.

Afternoon: Savor a leisurely brunch at the French Press, renowned for its delectable pastries and aromatic coffee. Afterward, explore the trendy boutiques and eclectic shops lining State Street, Santa Barbara's vibrant shopping district.

Evening: As your Santa Barbara adventure comes to an end, indulge in a farewell dinner at the Black Sheep, where innovative cuisine and a lively atmosphere await. Savor the flavors of Santa Barbara, reminisce about the unforgettable experiences, and cherish the memories created in this coastal paradise.

2.7 7 Days Itinerary Planning

Day 1:

Start your day with a visit to the Santa Barbara Courthouse, a Spanish Colonial Revival landmark that offers stunning views of the city and the coastline.

Take a stroll along Stearns Wharf, a pier lined with shops, restaurants, and cafes.

Enjoy lunch at one of the many waterfront restaurants, such as the Harbor View Cafe or the Brophy Brothers Fish Market.

Spend the afternoon exploring the Santa Barbara Botanic Garden, home to a diverse collection of plants from around the world.

Day 2:

Start your day with a walk or bike ride along Leadbetter Beach, a popular spot for swimming, sunbathing, and surfing.

Visit the Santa Barbara Museum of Art, which houses a collection of American and European art.

Enjoy lunch at one of the many restaurants in the Funk Zone, a neighborhood known for its art galleries, boutiques, and wine tasting rooms.

Spend the afternoon at the Santa Barbara Zoo, where you can see animals from around the world, including lions, tigers, and bears.

Day 3:

Take a boat tour of the Channel Islands National Park, where you can see wildlife such as dolphins, whales, and seals.

Hike to the top of Inspiration Point, where you can enjoy panoramic views of the islands and the coastline.

Visit El Presidio de Santa Barbara State Historic Park, a former Spanish military fort that offers a glimpse into the city's history.

Enjoy dinner at one of the many restaurants in the downtown area, such as Bouchon or the Black Sheep.

Day 4:

Visit the Old Mission Santa Barbara, a Franciscan mission founded in 1786.

Take a walk or bike ride along the Mission Creek Trail, a scenic route that winds through the city.

Visit the Santa Barbara Museum of Natural History, which houses a collection of exhibits on the natural history of the region.

Enjoy dinner at one of the many restaurants in the Funk Zone, such as The Bear and the Star or the Lucky Llama.

Day 5:

Visit Ganna Walska Lotusland, a beautiful garden that is home to a collection of lotus flowers and other plants from around the world.

Take a tour of Casa del Herrero, a Spanish Colonial Revival mansion with stunning ocean views.

Spend the afternoon at Refugio State Beach, a popular spot for swimming, sunbathing, and surfing.

Enjoy dinner at one of the many restaurants in the town of Carpinteria, such as the Seagrass Restaurant or the Casanova Restaurant.

Day 6:

Visit Gaviota State Park, a popular spot for hiking, camping, and fishing.

Spend the afternoon at Jalama Beach, a secluded spot with stunning ocean views.

Visit Chumash Painted Cave State Historic Park, where you can see ancient pictographs painted by the Chumash people.

Enjoy dinner at one of the many restaurants in the town of Solvang, such as the Danish Mill Bakery or the Solvang Restaurant.

Day 7:

Take a leisurely drive along the Pacific Coast Highway, enjoying the stunning scenery.

Visit Hearst Castle, a lavish mansion built by newspaper magnate William Randolph Hearst.

Spend the afternoon at Moonstone Beach, a popular spot for tidepooling, swimming, and sunbathing.

Enjoy dinner at one of the many restaurants in the town of Cambria, such as the Cambria Pines Lodge or the Moonstone Beach Bar & Grill.

This itinerary is just a suggestion, of course, and you can tailor it to your own interests and preferences. I hope you have a wonderful time in Santa Barbara!

NOTE

CHAPTER THREE

Getting There

3.1 By Air

The closest airport to Santa Barbara is Santa Barbara Municipal Airport (SBA), located just 8 miles from the city center.

Nonstop flights to Santa Barbara

Alaska Airlines: Seattle (SEA) and Portland (PDX)

American Airlines: Dallas (DFW) and Phoenix (PHX)

Delta Air Lines: Salt Lake City (SLC)

Southwest Airlines: Las Vegas (LAS), Phoenix (PHX), and San Francisco (SFO)

United Airlines: Denver (DEN), Los Angeles (LAX), San Francisco (SFO), and San Jose (SJC)

Other airports near Santa Barbara

Burbank (BUR): 78.9 miles away

Los Angeles (LAX): 81.2 miles away

Santa Ana (SNA): 117.7 miles away

Ontario/San Bernardino (ONT): 123.2 miles away

Ground transportation from the airport

Taxi: The taxi stand is located outside the terminal building. The cost of a taxi ride to the city center is approximately $30.

Ride-sharing: Uber and Lyft are both available at SBA Airport. The cost of a ride to the city center is approximately $20.

Public bus: The Santa Barbara Metropolitan Transit District (MTD) operates Route 11 from the airport to the city center. The fare is $1.50.

Shuttle: There are several shuttle companies that offer transportation from the airport to Santa Barbara hotels. The cost of a shuttle ride is approximately $20.

Tips for flying to Santa Barbara

- Book your flights in advance, especially if you are traveling during peak season.

- Arrive at the airport at least two hours before your flight departure time.

- Check in for your flight online or at the kiosks in the terminal.

- Have your boarding pass and identification ready when you go through security.

- Pack light to avoid baggage fees.

3.2 By Car

The drive from San Francisco to Santa Barbara is approximately 325 miles and takes about 5 hours and 11 minutes. The route is mostly along the scenic US-101 highway, which hugs the California coast.

Direction Tips

- Start in San Francisco and head south on US-101.

- Continue on US-101 for about 190 miles, passing through San Jose, Monterey, and Carmel-by-the-Sea.

- In San Luis Obispo, take Exit 180A to merge onto CA-166 East.

- Follow CA-166 East for about 25 miles, passing through Pismo Beach and Arroyo Grande.

- In Guadalupe, take Exit 147 to merge onto CA-101 South.

- Continue on CA-101 South for about 30 miles until you reach Santa Barbara.

Here are some additional tips for driving to Santa Barbara:

- Be aware of the speed limits. The speed limit on US-101 is typically 65 mph, but it can be lower in some areas.

- Be prepared for traffic. Traffic can be heavy on US-101, especially during peak hours.

- Allow extra time for your trip. If you are driving during the summer, be sure to allow extra time for traffic and stops at popular tourist destinations.

3.3 By Train

Getting to Santa Barbara by train is a wonderful way to enjoy the scenic beauty of the California coast.

The Pacific Surfliner is a passenger train service that runs between San Diego and San Luis Obispo, with stops in Santa Barbara. It offers six trains per day in each direction, so you can easily find a schedule that fits your needs. The Pacific Surfliner travels along the Pacific Ocean for much of its route, offering stunning views of the coastline. The trip from Los Angeles to Santa Barbara takes about 2 hours and 30 minutes, while the trip from San Diego to Santa Barbara takes about 4 hours.

Coast Starlight

The Coast Starlight is a long-distance passenger train service that runs between Los Angeles and Seattle, with stops in Santa Barbara. It offers one train per day in each direction. The Coast Starlight travels inland for the first part of its route, but it eventually merges with the Pacific Surfliner and follows the coastline along the way. The trip from Los Angeles to Santa Barbara takes about 3 hours and 30 minutes, while the trip from Seattle to Santa Barbara takes about 30 hours.

Ticketing and Reservations

You can purchase tickets for either train online or at the Amtrak station. Reservations are recommended, especially for travel during peak season.

Tips for Taking the Train to Santa Barbara

- Arrive at the station at least 30 minutes before your train departs.

- Check the train schedule carefully to make sure you are taking the right train.

- If you are traveling with luggage, be sure to check the Amtrak baggage policy.

- Bring snacks and drinks on board with you, as there is no food service on the train.

- Relax and enjoy the scenic views!

CHAPTER FOUR

Accommodation Options

4.1 Hotels

Santa Barbara, nestled along the picturesque Californian coast, is renowned for its stunning beaches, Spanish colonial architecture, and charming atmosphere. Whether you're seeking a luxurious seaside escape or a budget-friendly retreat, Santa Barbara offers an array of hotels to suit every traveler's needs and preferences.

Luxury Hotels for an Unforgettable Experience

Indulge in the epitome of luxury at these Santa Barbara hotels, where every detail is meticulously crafted to pamper and delight discerning guests.

Hotel Californian: Embrace coastal elegance at Hotel Californian, a AAA Four-Diamond resort boasting stylish accommodations, oceanfront dining, and a rooftop terrace with mesmerizing views. Price range: $350 - $900 per night.

Kimpton Canary Hotel: Experience refined sophistication at Kimpton Canary Hotel, featuring spacious rooms with plush amenities, a rooftop pool with panoramic city views, and complimentary perks like an evening wine hour. Price range: $400 - $700 per night.

Hotel Santa Barbara: Immerse yourself in Spanish colonial grandeur at Hotel Santa Barbara, a historic landmark offering opulent accommodations, renowned dining venues, and a rejuvenating spa. Price range: $500 - $1,000 per night.

Mid-Range Hotels for Comfort and Convenience

Discover a balance of comfort, affordability, and prime locations at these mid-range Santa Barbara hotels, perfect for those seeking a delightful yet value-conscious stay.

The Harbor View Inn: Enjoy a beachfront haven at The Harbor View Inn, where cozy rooms with ocean views, a picturesque harbor setting, and a friendly atmosphere await. Price range: $200 - $400 per night.

Beachside Inn: Embrace the laid-back Californian vibe at Beachside Inn, offering comfortable accommodations, a relaxed outdoor pool area, and easy access to the beach. Price range: $150 - $300 per night.

Avania Inn of Santa Barbara: Experience a blend of comfort and convenience at Avania Inn of Santa Barbara, featuring spacious rooms, a sparkling outdoor pool, and a convenient location near downtown attractions. Price range: $100 - $250 per night.

Budget-Friendly Hotels for a Cost-Effective Stay

Enjoy a Santa Barbara getaway without breaking the bank at these budget-friendly hotels, providing clean, comfortable accommodations without compromising on essential amenities.

Castillo Inn at the Beach: Immerse yourself in a charming beachside setting at Castillo Inn at the Beach, offering basic yet comfortable rooms, a shared kitchen, and a laid-back atmosphere. Price range: $75 - $150 per night.

The Franciscan Hotel: Experience the charm of Old Town at The Franciscan Hotel, featuring historic architecture, cozy rooms, and a convenient location near shops, restaurants, and attractions. Price range: $50 - $100 per night.

Motel 6 Santa Barbara, CA - Beach: Enjoy a simple yet affordable stay at Motel 6 Santa Barbara, CA - Beach, offering clean rooms, a convenient location near the beach, and a budget-friendly price tag. Price range: $50 - $100 per night.

Whether you seek luxurious pampering, comfortable convenience, or budget-friendly charm, Santa Barbara's diverse hotel landscape caters to every traveler's desires. Embrace the coastal allure of this captivating Californian city and discover the perfect hotel to complement your unforgettable Santa Barbara experience.

4.2 Bed And Breakfasts

Escape to the enchanting realm of Santa Barbara, where charming bed and breakfasts provide a haven of personalized hospitality and intimate ambiance. Immerse yourself in the tranquil beauty of these meticulously curated accommodations, each offering a unique blend of style, comfort, and personalized service.

Luxurious Retreats for an Unforgettable Getaway

Indulge in the epitome of luxury at these Santa Barbara bed and breakfasts, where every detail is meticulously crafted to provide an unforgettable getaway.

Inn at East Beach: Experience coastal elegance at Inn at East Beach, a AAA Five-Diamond bed and breakfast boasting luxurious accommodations, panoramic ocean views, and a gourmet breakfast. Price range: $400 - $800 per night.

Lavender Inn by the Sea: Embrace Mediterranean charm at Lavender Inn by the Sea, featuring individually decorated rooms, a tranquil garden courtyard, and a complimentary gourmet breakfast. Price range: $300 - $600 per night.

Secret Garden Inn & Cottages: Discover a hidden oasis at Secret Garden Inn & Cottages, offering individually decorated rooms, a lush garden retreat, and a delectable breakfast prepared with fresh, local ingredients. Price range: $250 - $500 per night.

Charming Enclaves for a Tranquil Stay

Embrace the charm and tranquility of these Santa Barbara bed and breakfasts, where every corner exudes warmth and personalized attention.

Casa Del Mar Inn: Immerse yourself in Spanish colonial charm at Casa Del Mar Inn, featuring warm, inviting rooms, a tranquil courtyard garden, and a complimentary European-style breakfast. Price range: $200 - $400 per night.

Villa Rosa Inn: Experience the allure of Old California at Villa Rosa Inn, offering polished rooms, a lounge for social gatherings, a sparkling pool, and a hot tub for relaxation. Price range: $150 - $300 per night.

The Eagle Inn: Discover a piece of history at The Eagle Inn, a restored Victorian mansion featuring elegant rooms with period details, a cozy parlor, and a delightful breakfast. Price range: $100 - $200 per night.

Budget-Friendly Gems for a Cozy Escape

Enjoy a cozy and affordable retreat at these Santa Barbara bed and breakfasts, where comfort and hospitality meet value.

Harbor House Inn: Embrace the seaside charm at Harbor House Inn, offering comfortable rooms with ocean views, a shared kitchen, and a friendly atmosphere. Price range: $75 - $150 per night.

Sandpiper Inn: Experience the laid-back Californian vibe at Sandpiper Inn, featuring cozy rooms, a shared kitchen, and easy access to the beach. Price range: $50 - $100 per night.

Avila Beach Inn: Discover a charming retreat at Avila Beach Inn, offering simple yet comfortable rooms, a shared kitchen, and a convenient location near the beach. Price range: $50 - $100 per night.

Indulge in the unique charm and personalized hospitality of Santa Barbara's bed and breakfasts. Whether you seek luxurious pampering, tranquil ambiance, or budget-friendly comfort, these havens of rest and relaxation will enhance your Santa Barbara experience with timeless elegance and heartfelt service.

4.3 Vacation Rentals

Santa Barbara, nestled along California's picturesque coastline, beckons travelers with its captivating blend of natural beauty, Spanish colonial heritage, and vibrant cultural scene. Whether you crave beachfront bliss, urban convenience, or a tranquil retreat, Santa Barbara's diverse array of vacation rentals caters to every preference and budget.

Seaside Getaways for Oceanfront Living

Embrace the allure of the Pacific Ocean at these Santa Barbara vacation rentals, where the soothing rhythm of the waves and the salty tang of the sea air await.

Beachfront Bliss: Indulge in beachfront luxury at these opulent vacation rentals, offering direct access to the sandy shores, panoramic ocean views, and lavish amenities. Price range: $500 - $1,500 per night.

Surfside Serenity: Discover cozy cottage retreats nestled just steps from the beach, providing an intimate escape with the soothing sounds of the waves and the gentle sea breeze. Price range: $200 - $500 per night.

Beach Bum Haven: Embrace the laid-back coastal lifestyle at these casual beachfront rentals, offering comfortable accommodations, easy access to the beach, and an unpretentious atmosphere. Price range: $100 - $300 per night.

Downtown Charm for Urban Adventures

Immerse yourself in the heart of Santa Barbara's vibrant downtown at these vacation rentals, offering convenient access to shops, restaurants, and cultural attractions.

Urban Oasis: Experience the city's energy from these stylish downtown rentals, featuring modern amenities, rooftop terraces with city views, and a lively atmosphere. Price range: $300 - $600 per night.

Historic Charm: Discover the city's rich heritage in these restored historic rentals, offering a blend of old-world charm, modern conveniences, and a unique sense of character. Price range: $200 - $400 per night.

Downtown Retreat: Embrace the convenience of these cozy downtown rentals, providing a comfortable base for exploring the city's attractions, with easy access to public transportation and amenities. Price range: $100 - $250 per night.

Tranquil Escapes for Mountain Serenity

Find solace amidst the foothills and vineyards of the Santa Ynez Mountains at these vacation rentals, offering a serene escape from the hustle and bustle.

Hilltop Haven: Indulge in panoramic views and tranquil surroundings at these luxurious hilltop rentals, featuring private pools, spacious gardens, and a sense of seclusion. Price range: $400 - $800 per night.

Vineyard Retreat: Immerse yourself in the heart of Santa Barbara's renowned wine country at these charming vineyard rentals, offering rustic elegance, breathtaking vineyard views, and a taste of the region's finest wines. Price range: $200 - $500 per night.

Countryside Serenity: Discover a peaceful retreat at these cozy countryside rentals, nestled amidst rolling hills, verdant landscapes, and a tranquil atmosphere. Price range: $100 - $300 per night.

Whether you seek the invigorating energy of the coast, the vibrant pulse of the city, or the serenity of the countryside, Santa Barbara's vacation rentals offer a diverse tapestry of accommodations to suit every traveler's desires. Embrace the unique charm and endless possibilities that Santa Barbara has to offer, and find your perfect vacation rental haven.

NOTE

_____

_____

_____

_____

_____

_____

_____

_____

_____

_____

CHAPTER FIVE

Downtown Santa Barbara

5.1 State Street

State Street is a vibrant pedestrian thoroughfare that serves as the heart of Santa Barbara's downtown. This palm-lined street is home to an eclectic mix of shops, restaurants, and attractions, making it a popular destination for locals and visitors alike.

Shopping

State Street is a shopper's paradise, with a wide variety of stores to suit every taste and budget. From high-end boutiques to local artisan shops, you're sure to find something unique and special here. Some of the most popular stores on State Street include:

- Anthropologie

- The RealReal

- Lush Cosmetics

- Patagonia

- Apple

- Restaurants

State Street is also home to a diverse array of restaurants, serving everything from fresh seafood to authentic Mexican cuisine. Here are a few of our favorites:

- The Habit Burger Grill

- McConnell's Ice Cream

- The Black Sheep

- The Lark

- Heirsloom

- Attractions

In addition to shopping and dining, State Street is also home to a number of popular attractions, including:

- The Santa Barbara County Courthouse

- The Santa Barbara Museum of Art

- The Funk Zone

- Stearns Wharf

- Santa Barbara Harbor

- Events

State Street is also host to a number of popular events throughout the year, including:

- The Santa Barbara International Film Festival

- The Santa Barbara County Fair

- The Santa Barbara Parade of Lights

Getting to State Street

State Street is located in the heart of downtown Santa Barbara, and it is easy to get to by car, public transportation, or bike.

By car: State Street is easily accessible from Highway 101. There is also plenty of parking available in the area.

By public transportation: The Santa Barbara MTD bus system has a number of routes that stop on State Street.

By bike: State Street is a great way to get around Santa Barbara by bike. There is a dedicated bike lane on the street, and there are also a number of bike rental shops in the area.

State Street is a must-visit destination for anyone spending time in Santa Barbara. With its vibrant mix of shops, restaurants, and attractions, there is something for everyone to enjoy.

5.2 Historic Landmarks

Santa Barbara is renowned for its rich history and stunning architecture, with a collection of historic landmarks that offer a glimpse into the city's past. These landmarks range from grand Spanish Colonial buildings to charming Victorian houses, each with its unique story to tell. Let's explore some of the most notable historic landmarks in Santa Barbara:

Old Mission Santa Barbara

Founded in 1786 by Franciscan missionaries, the Old Mission Santa Barbara stands as a testament to the city's Spanish heritage. This iconic landmark features twin bell towers, a serene mission garden, and a museum showcasing artifacts from the mission's past. Visitors can tour the mission grounds, attend mass in the historic chapel, and learn about the Chumash people, the original inhabitants of the area.

Santa Barbara County Courthouse

Standing majestically on a hilltop overlooking the city, the Santa Barbara County Courthouse is a masterpiece of Spanish Colonial Revival architecture. Designed by renowned architect William Curlett, the courthouse was built in 1929 and features a sandstone façade, a clock tower, and a rooftop loggia with panoramic views of the city and coastline.

Casa de la Guerra

Step back in time at Casa de la Guerra, a beautifully preserved adobe hacienda that served as the residence of José de la Guerra, a prominent figure in Santa Barbara's Mexican and early American periods. Built in 1827, the hacienda features thick adobe walls, red-tiled roofs, and interior courtyards. Visitors can tour the house, furnished with period pieces, and imagine the lively gatherings that once took place within its walls.

Presidio de Santa Bárbara State Historic Park

Established in 1782, the Presidio de Santa Bárbara was the first Spanish military outpost in California. Today, the Presidio is a state historic park, offering visitors a glimpse into the lives of Spanish soldiers and their families. Explore the adobe barracks, the chapel, and the blacksmith shop, and imagine the daily activities that took place here over two centuries ago.

Moreton Bay Fig Tree

Standing at the corner of State and Carrillo streets, the Moreton Bay Fig Tree is a Santa Barbara icon. This magnificent tree, planted in 1877, boasts a sprawling canopy that provides shade and a sense of tranquility amidst the bustling downtown area. The tree is a popular spot for locals and visitors alike to gather and enjoy the outdoors.

These historic landmarks are just a few of the many that can be found in Santa Barbara. By exploring these treasured sites, visitors can gain a deeper appreciation for the city's rich history and cultural heritage.

CHAPTER SIX

Beaches And Parks

6.1 East Beach

Santa Barbara East Beach is a beautiful and popular beach located in Santa Barbara, California. The beach is known for its soft sand, clear water, and stunning views of the Santa Ynez Mountains. East Beach is also a great place to enjoy a variety of activities, such as swimming, sunbathing, surfing, and volleyball.

The beach is free to enter, but there is a fee for parking. Parking is available in a number of lots near the beach. There is also a metered parking lot on Shoreline Drive.

East Beach is a great place to spend a day at the beach. There are plenty of amenities to enjoy, such as restrooms, showers, and picnic tables. There is also a playground and a snack bar.

East Beach is a popular spot for swimming, sunbathing, and surfing. The waves at East Beach are typically gentle, making it a good spot for beginners. There are also a number of lifeguards on duty at the beach.

East Beach is also a great place to enjoy volleyball. There are over a dozen volleyball courts on the beach. There are also a number of leagues and tournaments held at East Beach throughout the year.

East Beach is a great place to relax and enjoy the outdoors. There are always a variety of people enjoying the beach, from families and friends to surfers and sunbathers.

If you are looking for a beautiful and popular beach to visit in Santa Barbara, East Beach is a great option.

6.2 West Beach

Nestled amidst the picturesque coastline of Santa Barbara, California, West Beach stands as a captivating haven for sun-seekers, adventure enthusiasts, and families alike. With its soft, golden sands, crystal-clear waters, and stunning backdrop of the Santa Ynez Mountains, West Beach offers an idyllic escape from the hustle and bustle of everyday life.

A Sanctuary for Leisure and Recreation

Stepping onto West Beach, visitors are greeted by an expanse of pristine shoreline, stretching for over a mile along the Pacific Ocean. The gentle waves lap against the shore, creating a soothing symphony that invites relaxation and tranquility. Sunbathers bask in the warmth of the Californian sun, while families gather under vibrant umbrellas, enjoying picnics and laughter-filled moments.

A Playground for Thrill-Seekers

For those seeking a more exhilarating experience, West Beach offers an array of water sports to ignite the senses. Surfers ride the waves with grace and agility, their boards slicing through the turquoise waters. Kayakers and paddleboarders glide effortlessly across the surface, exploring the hidden coves and inlets. And for those seeking a truly unique adventure, windsurfers harness the power of the wind, their colorful sails dancing against the azure sky.

A Vibrant Hub of Social Gatherings

As the sun dips towards the horizon, casting a warm glow over the beach, West Beach transforms into a vibrant hub of social gatherings. Volleyball enthusiasts gather on the designated courts, their cheers echoing through the air as they engage in friendly competitions. Meanwhile, families and friends gather around crackling bonfires, sharing stories and laughter under the starlit sky.

A Treasure Trove of Amenities and Conveniences

West Beach is not just a haven for recreation; it also boasts a wealth of amenities to cater to every need. Well-maintained restrooms and showers ensure a comfortable beach experience, while picnic tables provide ample space for alfresco dining. A playground filled with laughter and joyful squeals invites children to unleash their boundless energy. And for those seeking a quick bite, a snack bar offers refreshing treats and beverages.

A Gateway to Coastal Exploration

West Beach serves as an ideal starting point for exploring the captivating coastal wonders of Santa Barbara. The Cabrillo Boulevard bike path winds along the shoreline, offering breathtaking views of the Pacific Ocean and the Santa Ynez Mountains. Stearn's Wharf, a bustling waterfront destination, beckons with its fresh seafood eateries, souvenir shops, and lively atmosphere. And for a touch of history, the Santa Barbara Harbor, with its charming fishing boats and vibrant maritime culture, offers a glimpse into the city's rich past.

A Destination for All

Whether seeking a tranquil escape, an exhilarating adventure, or a vibrant social gathering, Santa Barbara West Beach seamlessly blends natural beauty with a plethora of activities and amenities, making it a haven for beachgoers of all ages and preferences. With its welcoming atmosphere and endless possibilities for fun and relaxation, West Beach is a true gem of the Californian coastline.

6.3 Parks And Gardens

Santa Barbara is renowned for its picturesque coastline and charming coastal towns, but it also harbors a treasure trove of parks and gardens that offer a tranquil retreat from the bustling city life. These verdant oases, adorned with vibrant blooms, lush greenery, and serene water features, provide a sanctuary for relaxation, exploration, and aesthetic delight.

Santa Barbara Botanic Garden: A Haven for Native Flora

Nestled amidst the foothills of the Santa Ynez Mountains, the Santa Barbara Botanic Garden is a haven for plant enthusiasts and nature lovers alike. This 150-acre botanical wonderland showcases a diverse collection of native California flora, meticulously arranged to represent the state's diverse ecosystems.

Visitors can wander through shady oak groves, stroll alongside meandering streams, and discover hidden gems like the serene Japanese Garden.

Ganna Walska Lotusland: A Symphony of Lotus Blooms

Perched atop the hills overlooking Santa Barbara, Ganna Walska Lotusland is a captivating retreat renowned for its breathtaking collection of lotus flowers. This 80-acre estate, once the home of Polish opera singer Madame Ganna Walska, is now a botanical masterpiece adorned with over 2,000 different plant species, including a mesmerizing pond filled with over 200 varieties of lotus.

Casa del Herrero: A Mediterranean Oasis

Immerse yourself in the grandeur of a Mediterranean estate at Casa del Herrero, a luxurious mansion surrounded by 12 acres of meticulously manicured gardens. This architectural marvel, inspired by Spanish and Italian Renaissance design, features a breathtaking central courtyard, adorned with cascading fountains, vibrant bougainvillea, and fragrant citrus trees.

Old Mission Santa Barbara: A Historic Gem with Serene Gardens

Step back in time at the Old Mission Santa Barbara, a historic Franciscan mission founded in 1786. This iconic landmark, known for its twin bell towers and serene architecture, also boasts a beautifully landscaped garden. Stroll through the tranquil Mission Rose Garden, lined with fragrant blooms, or relax beneath the shade of olive trees in the Mission Orchard.

Alice Keck Park Memorial Garden: A Tranquil Oasis

Located in the heart of Santa Barbara, Alice Keck Park Memorial Garden offers a tranquil escape from the city's hustle and bustle. This peaceful oasis, adorned with a meandering stream, cascading waterfalls, and a variety of blooming plants, provides a serene atmosphere for reflection and relaxation. Visitors can stroll through the garden's winding paths, enjoy a picnic under the shade of trees, or simply bask in the tranquility of nature.

NOTE

_____

_____

_____

_____

CHAPTER SEVEN

Cultural Attractions

7.1 Museums

Encompassing a vast collection of over 30,000 artworks spanning various cultures and periods, the SBMA is a must-visit for art enthusiasts. From ancient Mediterranean artifacts to contemporary American paintings, the museum's galleries offer a captivating journey through the history of art.

Entry Fee:

$15 for General Admission

$12 for Seniors (65+)

Free for Members and Children under 12

Opening and Closing Hours:

Wednesday - Sunday: 11 AM - 5 PM

Closed on Mondays and Tuesdays

Santa Barbara Museum of Natural History (SBMNH):
Delve into the wonders of the natural world at the SBMNH, where interactive exhibits and captivating displays bring science to life. Explore the prehistoric world through dinosaur fossils, discover the diverse ecosystems of the Santa Barbara Channel, and marvel at the wonders of space exploration.

Entry Fee:

$18 for General Admission

$16 for Seniors (65+)

$12 for Children (3-17)

Free for Members and Children under 3

Opening and Closing Hours:

Daily: 10 AM - 5 PM

Santa Barbara Maritime Museum (SBMM):

Embark on a voyage through maritime history at the SBMM, where artifacts, exhibits, and interactive displays chronicle the rich maritime heritage of Santa

Barbara. Explore ship models, learn about local maritime industries, and discover the stories of the people who shaped the city's seafaring legacy.

Entry Fee:

$15 for General Admission

$12 for Seniors (65+)

$10 for Students (with ID)

Free for Members and Children under 5

Opening and Closing Hours:

Thursday - Tuesday: 11 AM - 4 PM

Closed on Wednesdays

MOXI, The Wolf Museum of Exploration + Innovation:

Spark curiosity and ignite imaginations at MOXI, an interactive museum designed for children and families. Through hands-on exhibits, engaging workshops, and stimulating programs, MOXI encourages exploration, creativity, and a love for learning in a fun and engaging environment.

Entry Fee:

$20 for General Admission

$18 for Seniors (65+)

$16 for Children (1-17)

Free for Members and Infants under 1

Opening and Closing Hours:

Daily: 10 AM - 5 PM

7.2 Art Galleries

Santa Barbara is home to a vibrant arts scene, with a wide variety of art galleries to explore. From contemporary art to traditional American art, there's something for everyone to enjoy. Here are a few of the most popular art galleries in Santa Barbara, along with their entry fees, opening and closing hours.

Santa Barbara Museum of Art is one of the largest and most respected art museums in California. The museum houses a collection of over 12,000 works of art, spanning from ancient times to the present day. The museum also hosts a variety of special exhibitions and events throughout the year.

Entry fee: Free

Opening hours: Tuesday-Sunday, 11 am to 5 pm

Closed: Mondays

Sullivan Goss – An American Gallery Sullivan Goss – An American Gallery is a premier gallery specializing in American art from the late 19th and early 20th centuries. The gallery's collection includes works by some of the most famous American artists, including Winslow Homer, Charles Burchfield, and Georgia O'Keeffe.

Entry fee: Free

Opening hours: Tuesday-Saturday, 10 am to 5 pm

Closed: Sundays and Mondays

10 West Gallery is a contemporary art gallery that showcases the work of emerging and established artists. The gallery's exhibitions are always changing, so there's always something new to see.

Entry fee: Free
Opening hours: Tuesday-Saturday, 11 am to 5 pm

Closed: Sundays and Mondays

Santa Barbara Fine Art Gallery is a commercial gallery that represents a wide variety of artists, from local up-and-coming artists to established international artists. The gallery's exhibitions are always curated with a focus on quality and innovation.

Entry fee: Free

Opening hours: Monday-Saturday, 10 am to 5 pm

Closed: Sundays

Museum of Contemporary Art Santa Barbara The Museum of Contemporary Art Santa Barbara is a non-profit museum that is dedicated to collecting, exhibiting, and interpreting contemporary art. The museum's collection includes works by some of the most important contemporary artists, including Andy Warhol, Jeff Koons, and Cindy Sherman.

Entry fee: $10 for adults, $5 for students and seniors

Opening hours: Wednesday-Sunday, 11 am to 5 pm

Closed: Tuesdays

In addition to these popular galleries, there are many other smaller galleries and art spaces worth exploring in Santa Barbara. So take some time to wander through the city's art scene and discover something new.

7.3 Performing Arts

Santa Barbara is a vibrant hub for the performing arts, offering a diverse range of theatrical productions, musical performances, and dance recitals throughout the year. From intimate venues to grand theaters, the city caters to various tastes and preferences, providing captivating experiences for art enthusiasts.

The Granada Theatre, a Spanish Colonial Revival landmark, stands as the crown jewel of Santa Barbara's performing arts scene. Built in 1924, the theater has hosted a legendary array of performers, from Broadway productions to world-renowned orchestras. Its opulent interior, featuring gold leaf accents and intricate murals, creates an ambiance of elegance and grandeur.

Entry fee: Varies depending on the performance

Opening hours: Box office hours: Monday-Friday, 12 pm to 5 pm. Performance times vary.
Closed: Closed on Sundays and select Mondays

Lobero Theatre Nestled in the heart of Santa Barbara's historic downtown, the Lobero Theatre exudes a rich cultural heritage. Constructed in 1873, it is the oldest continuously operating performing arts venue in California. The theater's intimate setting and exceptional acoustics provide an immersive experience for audiences.

Entry fee: Varies depending on the performance

Opening hours: Box office hours: Monday-Saturday, 12 pm to 5 pm. Performance times vary.

Closed: Closed on Sundays

Arlington Theatre, a majestic landmark on State Street, serves as a vibrant entertainment hub. Originally built in 1931 as a movie palace, the theater has since transformed into a versatile venue hosting a variety of performances, from Broadway shows to concerts and film screenings. Its Art Deco architecture and spacious interior create a captivating atmosphere.

Entry fee: Varies depending on the performance

Opening hours: Box office hours: Monday-Saturday, 12 pm to 5 pm. Performance times vary.

Closed: Closed on Sundays

Ensemble Theatre Company, a resident company at the New Vic Theatre, presents a diverse repertoire of thought-provoking and engaging theatrical productions. From classical dramas to contemporary plays, the company's productions challenge and inspire audiences, fostering a deeper appreciation for the performing arts.

Entry fee: Varies depending on the performance

Opening hours: Box office hours: Tuesday-Saturday, 1 pm to 5 pm. Performance times vary.

Closed: Closed on Sundays and Mondays

CAMA Santa Barbara, the Community Arts Music Association, brings world-class classical music performances to Santa Barbara. Since 1952, CAMA has presented renowned orchestras, chamber ensembles, and soloists, enriching the city's cultural landscape.

Entry fee: Varies depending on the performance

Opening hours: Performance times vary.
Closed: No fixed closure days.

These are just a few of the many performing arts venues and organizations that contribute to Santa Barbara's vibrant cultural scene. With its diverse offerings and captivating performances, Santa Barbara provides an unforgettable experience for art lovers seeking to immerse themselves in the world of theater, music, and dance.

NOTE

_____

_____

_____

_____

_____

CHAPTER EIGHT

Outdoor Activities

8.1 Hiking And Trails

Nestled along the picturesque Californian coastline, Santa Barbara is a haven for outdoor enthusiasts, offering a diverse range of hiking trails that cater to all skill levels and interests. From leisurely strolls along the oceanfront to challenging ascents into the verdant Santa Ynez Mountains, Santa Barbara's hiking trails provide an unparalleled opportunity to immerse oneself in the region's natural beauty and rich history.

Coastal Trails for Panoramic Views

For those seeking breathtaking ocean vistas, Santa Barbara's coastal trails offer an unforgettable experience. The Douglas Family Preserve, located just steps from the beach, boasts panoramic views of the Pacific Ocean, while the Shoreline Park Trail winds its way along the sandy shores, providing a tranquil escape from the bustling city.

Mountain Trails for Adventure Seekers

Venturing inland, the Santa Ynez Mountains beckon with their rugged terrain and exhilarating climbs. Inspiration Point Trail, a moderately challenging route, rewards hikers with stunning views of the city and coastline from its namesake summit. For a more strenuous adventure, the Rattlesnake Canyon Trail ascends through dense oak forests, leading to cascading waterfalls and hidden swimming holes.

Waterfall Trails for a Refreshing Retreat

Santa Barbara's hiking trails are not only renowned for their scenic beauty but also for their refreshing waterfalls. The Seven Falls Trail, a popular destination, features a series of cascading waterfalls that provide a welcome respite from the warm Californian sun. For a more secluded experience, the Tangerine Falls Trail leads to a hidden waterfall tucked away in the heart of the mountains.

Hidden Gems for Tranquility

Beyond the well-trodden paths, Santa Barbara harbors hidden gems that offer a tranquil escape from the crowds. The Jesusita Trail, a moderately challenging route, winds through oak groves and grasslands, providing a glimpse into the region's diverse ecosystem. For a more secluded adventure, the Cold Spring Loop offers a tranquil escape, leading to a secluded swimming hole nestled amidst the lush greenery.

Santa Barbara's hiking trails are not merely paths through nature; they are gateways to adventure, discovery, and self-reflection. Whether seeking panoramic coastal views, challenging mountain climbs, or refreshing waterfall retreats, Santa Barbara's trails offer an unparalleled opportunity to connect with the region's natural splendor and create lasting memories.

8.2 Water Activities

8.2.1 Kayaking

Santa Barbara, California, is a paradise for kayaking enthusiasts, offering a diverse range of experiences to suit all skill levels and interests. From tranquil paddles along the sheltered harbor to exhilarating rides through the crashing waves of the Pacific, Santa Barbara's kayaking scene promises an unforgettable aquatic adventure.

Sheltered Harbor Kayaking: A Serene Escape

For beginners and those seeking a leisurely kayaking experience, Santa Barbara Harbor provides an ideal setting. The calm waters and protected coves offer a tranquil escape, allowing paddlers to glide effortlessly past sailboats, yachts, and fishing vessels. Along the way, kayakers can admire the vibrant marine life, including playful dolphins and majestic sea lions basking on the sun-drenched rocks.

Coastal Kayaking: Unveiling Hidden Beaches and Cove

Adventurous kayakers can embark on a thrilling journey along Santa Barbara's scenic coastline, exploring secluded beaches and hidden coves. The Gaviota Coast, stretching northwards from the city, offers a rugged and dramatic landscape, with towering cliffs plunging into the turquoise waters. As kayakers paddle along this rugged coastline, they may encounter playful sea otters frolicking in the kelp beds and majestic gray whales migrating along their coastal route.

Channel Islands Kayaking: A Wildlife Paradise

For experienced kayakers seeking an unforgettable adventure, the Channel Islands National Park, located off the coast of Santa Barbara, is a kayaker's paradise. These five remote islands, each with its unique ecosystem, offer a wealth of opportunities for exploration and wildlife encounters. Kayakers can paddle through kelp forests, teeming with marine life, and encounter playful

dolphins, curious harbor seals, and even majestic
humpback whales breaching the water.

Sunset Kayaking: A Magical Experience

As the sun dips below the horizon, casting a warm glow
over the Santa Barbara coastline, kayaking takes on a
magical dimension. Sunset kayaking tours offer a serene
and unforgettable experience, allowing paddlers to
witness the transformation of the landscape as the sky
ignites with hues of orange, pink, and purple. The
tranquil waters reflect the vibrant colors, creating a
mesmerizing spectacle that leaves kayakers in awe of
nature's beauty.

8.2.2 Surfing

Santa Barbara, California, is a renowned surfing
destination, attracting wave riders from around the world
to experience its world-class swells and legendary surf
breaks. With its consistent surf conditions, diverse range
of breaks, and stunning coastal scenery, Santa Barbara
offers an unforgettable surfing experience for surfers of
all skill levels.

Rincon Point: The Queen of the Coast

Rincon Point, arguably Santa Barbara's most iconic surf break, is a legendary longboarder's paradise. The gently peeling waves, rolling for up to half a mile, have earned Rincon Point the title of "The Queen of the Coast." Advanced surfers can carve out long, graceful turns, while longboarders can showcase their mastery of classic maneuvers.

Leadbetter Point: A Challenge for Experienced Surfers

Leadbetter Point, located just south of Rincon Point, is a challenging and rewarding surf break that attracts experienced surfers seeking thrilling rides. The consistent south swells produce powerful waves that form steep barrels, testing surfers' skills and pushing them to their limits. Only experienced surfers should venture into Leadbetter Point, as the powerful waves and strong currents can pose a serious challenge.

Campus Point: A Beginner-Friendly Surf Spot

Campus Point, situated near the University of California, Santa Barbara (UCSB), offers a gentler introduction to surfing. The smaller, more mellow waves provide a suitable learning environment for beginners to hone their skills and gain confidence in the water. Surf schools operate at Campus Point, offering lessons and rentals for those eager to experience the thrill of riding the waves.

El Capitan State Beach: A Versatile Surf Spot

El Capitan State Beach, with its diverse range of breaks, caters to surfers of all levels. The main break, known as El Capitan Reef, offers a mix of long, rolling waves and occasional barrels, suitable for intermediate to advanced surfers. For beginners, the inside reef provides smaller, more manageable waves for practice and progression.

Sands: A Relaxing Surf Experience

Sands, located just east of El Capitan State Beach, offers a more relaxed surfing experience. The gently rolling waves and sandy bottom make Sands a popular spot for beginners and longboarders. The mellow atmosphere and consistent waves create an ideal setting for enjoying the tranquility of surfing.

Santa Barbara's surfing scene extends beyond these iconic breaks, with numerous other spots scattered along the coastline, each offering its unique character and challenges. Whether seeking the thrill of conquering powerful waves or the serenity of gliding through gentle swells, Santa Barbara's diverse surf breaks provide an unforgettable experience for surfers of all levels.

8.2.3 Whale Watching

Santa Barbara, California, is a renowned whale-watching destination, offering a unique opportunity to witness these majestic marine giants in their natural habitat. The nutrient-rich waters off the Santa Barbara Channel attract a diverse array of whale species, making it one of the most prolific whale-watching destinations in the world.

A Haven for Diverse Whale Species

The Santa Barbara Channel serves as a vital migratory corridor for numerous whale species, providing them with abundant food sources and sheltered coves during their seasonal migrations. Gray whales, known for their acrobatic leaps and tail lobs, are frequently spotted during their southbound migration from February to May, while humpback whales, renowned for their haunting songs, can be observed from May to November as they breach and lunge-feed on krill.

Diverse Whale-Watching Excursions

Santa Barbara offers a variety of whale-watching excursions to cater to different preferences and budgets. Experienced whale-watching operators conduct guided tours aboard spacious catamarans or smaller inflatables, providing expert commentary and insights into the behaviors and conservation of these marine giants. These tours typically depart from Santa Barbara Harbor and venture into the Santa Barbara Channel, where the likelihood of encountering whales is high.

An Unforgettable Encounter with Nature

Whale-watching excursions in Santa Barbara offer an unforgettable opportunity to connect with nature and witness the awe-inspiring beauty of these majestic creatures. As whales breach, spyhop, and display their massive tail flukes, onlookers are filled with a sense of wonder and appreciation for the diversity and power of the marine world.

Conservation Efforts for a Thriving Marine Ecosystem

Whale-watching operators in Santa Barbara are committed to responsible ecotourism practices, ensuring that their activities minimize any impact on the marine environment. They adhere to strict guidelines to avoid disturbing the whales' natural behaviors and contribute to the conservation of these endangered species.

A Rewarding Experience for All Ages

Whale-watching excursions in Santa Barbara are a rewarding experience for all ages, offering an opportunity to learn about marine conservation and create lasting memories. Children are particularly fascinated by the sight of these colossal creatures, sparking a lifelong interest in the natural world.

8.3 Biking

Santa Barbara, nestled along California's picturesque coastline, is a haven for cyclists of all levels. From leisurely coastal rides to challenging mountain biking trails, the city offers a diverse range of biking experiences that cater to every preference. Whether you're a seasoned rider or a casual enthusiast, Santa Barbara's biking trails promise an exhilarating and unforgettable adventure.

Coastal Cruising: A Breeze Along the Cabrillo Bike Path

For a scenic and relaxing ride, the Cabrillo Bike Path is an ideal choice. Stretching over three miles from Leadbetter Beach to Butterfly Beach, this paved path hugs the coastline, offering breathtaking views of the Pacific Ocean, Santa Ynez Mountains, and Channel Islands. The path is relatively flat and easy to navigate, making it perfect for families, casual riders, and those seeking a leisurely coastal cruise.

Mountain Biking Adventures: Elings Park and Jesusita Trail

For avid mountain bikers, Santa Barbara's terrain provides ample opportunities to test their skills and revel in the thrill of off-road riding. Elings Park, located just outside of downtown, offers a network of nine miles of well-maintained mountain biking trails, ranging from beginner-friendly to challenging climbs and descents. For a more challenging ride, the Jesusita Trail, a nine-mile loop trail, winds through the foothills of the Santa Ynez Mountains, offering panoramic views of the city and beyond.

Wine Country Tours: Pedaling Through Vineyards

Santa Barbara's renowned wine country is also a paradise for cyclists. Several companies offer guided wine country biking tours, allowing riders to explore the vineyards and savor the region's exceptional wines while enjoying the fresh air and scenic beauty. These tours typically include stops at several wineries, where participants can indulge in wine tastings and learn about the winemaking process.

Bike Rentals and Tours: Gearing Up for Adventure

Santa Barbara offers a variety of bike rental options, catering to both short-term and extended stays. Several shops rent a wide range of bikes, including road bikes, mountain bikes, and electric bikes. Additionally, guided biking tours are available for those seeking a more structured and informative experience.

Price Range for Bike Rentals and Tours:

Bike Rentals: Hourly rates typically range from $10 to $25, with daily rates ranging from $30 to $60.

Guided Biking Tours: Half-day tours typically range from $75 to $125, while full-day tours can range from $125 to $200.

Wine Country Tours: Guided wine country biking tours typically range from $100 to $150 per person, including bike rental, wine tastings, and lunch.

Whether you're seeking a leisurely coastal ride, an adrenaline-pumping mountain biking adventure, or a wine-tasting excursion, Santa Barbara's biking trails offer something for everyone. With its diverse terrain, stunning scenery, and abundance of bike rental and tour options, Santa Barbara is a true cyclist's paradise. So grab your bike, hit the trails, and discover the joys of cycling in this enchanting Californian gem.

8.4 Golf Courses

Santa Barbara, nestled along the picturesque Californian coastline, is a haven for golf enthusiasts, offering a diverse selection of courses that cater to all skill levels and preferences. From challenging championship layouts to scenic oceanfront courses, Santa Barbara's golf scene promises an unforgettable experience.

Sandpiper Golf Club: Perched atop dramatic cliffs overlooking the Pacific Ocean, Sandpiper Golf Club offers a breathtaking golfing experience. Designed by Robert Trent Jones Jr., the course features challenging doglegs, strategic water hazards, and stunning ocean views that will captivate even the most seasoned golfer. Green fees range from $185 to $250, depending on the day and time of play.

Glen Annie Golf Club: Nestled amidst the rolling foothills of Santa Ynez Mountains, Glen Annie Golf Club offers a tranquil escape from the hustle and bustle of city life. The course, designed by renowned golf architect Robert Trent Jones Sr., features a parkland layout with mature oak trees, meandering creeks, and picturesque ponds. Green fees range from $125 to $175, depending on the day and time of play.

Twin Lakes Golf Course: Located just minutes from downtown Santa Barbara, Twin Lakes Golf Course offers a challenging yet accessible golfing experience. The course features two distinct lakes, strategically placed bunkers, and undulating greens that demand precision and strategy. Green fees range from $80 to $120, depending on the day and time of play.

Montecito Country Club: Founded in 1916, Montecito Country Club is a private club that exudes elegance and tradition. The course, designed by Willie Watson and George C. Lyon, features rolling fairways, challenging bunkers, and stunning ocean views. Membership fees are undisclosed but are expected to be in the upper range.

Hidden Oaks Golf Club: Located in the heart of Santa Barbara's wine country, Hidden Oaks Golf Club offers a challenging yet enjoyable golfing experience. The course features mature oak trees, strategically placed water hazards, and undulating greens that demand accuracy and strategy. Green fees range from $120 to $160, depending on the day and time of play.

Rancho San Marcos Golf Course: Situated in the foothills of the Santa Ynez Mountains, Rancho San

Marcos Golf Club offers a picturesque setting for a memorable golfing experience. The course features a mix of parkland and links-style holes, challenging doglegs, and stunning mountain views. Green fees range from $80 to $120, depending on the day and time of play.

La Cumbre Country Club: Nestled amidst the foothills of the Santa Ynez Mountains, La Cumbre Country Club offers a tranquil escape from the hustle and bustle of city life. The course, designed by renowned golf architect Willie Watson, features a parkland layout with mature oak trees, meandering creeks, and picturesque ponds. Green fees are undisclosed but are expected to be in the upper range.

Valley Club of Montecito: Founded in 1928, Valley Club of Montecito is a private club that exudes elegance and tradition. The course, designed by George C. Lyon and William Flynn, features rolling fairways, challenging bunkers, and stunning ocean views. Membership fees are undisclosed but are expected to be in the upper range.

Birnam Wood Golf Club: Located just minutes from downtown Santa Barbara, Birnam Wood Golf Club offers a challenging yet accessible golfing experience. The course features two distinct lakes, strategically placed bunkers, and undulating greens that demand precision and strategy. Green fees range from $80 to $120, depending on the day and time of play.

Ocean Meadows Golf Course: Situated in the heart of Santa Barbara's wine country, Ocean Meadows Golf Course offers a picturesque setting for a memorable golfing experience. The course features a mix of parkland and links-style holes, challenging doglegs, and stunning ocean views. Green fees range from $80 to $120, depending on the day and time of play.

NOTE

CHAPTER NINE

Dining And Cuisine

9.1 Seafood

Santa Barbara, nestled along the picturesque Californian coastline, is renowned for its culinary treasures, particularly its fresh seafood bounty. From succulent shellfish to delicate finfish, Santa Barbara's seafood scene offers a diverse array of flavors and experiences to satisfy every palate.

Oysters: A Coastal Classic

No journey to Santa Barbara is complete without indulging in the city's iconic oysters. Harvested from local pristine waters, Santa Barbara oysters are known for their delicate briny flavor and creamy texture. The Santa Barbara Shellfish Company, located on Stearns Wharf, is a must-visit destination for oyster enthusiasts, offering a selection of local oysters served fresh on the half shell.

Price Range: $3-$5 per oyster

Shellfish: A Symphony of Flavors

Beyond oysters, Santa Barbara's seafood scene boasts an abundance of other shellfish delights. Dungeness crab, with its sweet, succulent meat, is a popular choice, often served steamed or cracked and served with garlic butter. For a taste of local delicacy, try the Santa Barbara spot prawns, known for their vibrant red shells and tender, sweet flesh.

Price Range:

Dungeness crab: $25-$35 per pound

Santa Barbara spot prawns: $30-$40 per pound

Finfish: A Culinary Canvas

Finfish lovers will find themselves spoiled for choice in Santa Barbara. Local favorites include grilled Santa Barbara halibut, known for its mild, buttery flavor, and pan-seared black cod, prized for its rich, meaty texture. For a taste of local pride, try the Santa Barbara swordfish, renowned for its firm, flavorful flesh.

Price Range:

Santa Barbara halibut: $25-$35 per pound

Black cod: $20-$30 per pound

Santa Barbara swordfish: $30-$40 per pound

Dining Experiences: From Casual to Upscale

Santa Barbara's seafood scene caters to a wide range of dining preferences. Casual waterfront eateries like the Santa Barbara FisHouse offer a relaxed atmosphere and stunning ocean views, while upscale establishments like The Harbor Restaurant provide a refined dining experience with impeccable service.

Price Range:

Casual waterfront eateries: $30-$50 per person

Upscale establishments: $50-$100 per person

Santa Barbara's seafood scene is a testament to the city's deep connection to the sea. With its fresh, locally sourced ingredients, diverse culinary offerings, and range of dining experiences, Santa Barbara offers an unforgettable seafood journey that will tantalize taste buds and create lasting memories.

9.2 Farm-to-Table

Santa Barbara, California, is renowned for its idyllic coastal setting, vibrant arts scene, and, of course, its delectable farm-to-table cuisine. Embracing the philosophy of sourcing ingredients from local farms and ranches, Santa Barbara's farm-to-table restaurants showcase the region's bounty, offering a symphony of flavors that celebrate the freshest produce and finest meats.

A Culinary Commitment to Freshness

Santa Barbara's farm-to-table movement is deeply rooted in a commitment to freshness and sustainability. Restaurants prioritize partnering with local farmers and ranchers, ensuring that ingredients travel the shortest distance from field to table, preserving their peak flavor and nutritional value. This emphasis on local sourcing also fosters a sense of community and environmental consciousness, reducing the carbon footprint associated with long-distance transportation.

A Culinary Adventure for Every Palate

Santa Barbara's farm-to-table restaurants cater to a diverse range of palates, offering an array of culinary experiences that showcase the region's rich agricultural heritage. From casual eateries to upscale establishments, each dining destination provides a unique perspective on farm-to-table cuisine.

Casual Delights: A Taste of the Land

For a taste of Santa Barbara's casual farm-to-table scene, venture to The Bear and Star, a rustic restaurant nestled amidst rolling hills. Their menu features seasonal dishes prepared with produce from their own ranch, offering a true farm-to-table experience. For a lighter bite, head to Scarlett Begonia, a charming café that serves up delectable brunch fare, showcasing fresh, local ingredients.

Price Range:

The Bear and Star: $30-$50 per person

Scarlett Begonia: $20-$30 per person

Upscale Elegance: A Culinary Symphony

For a more refined farm-to-table experience, indulge in the exquisite culinary creations at Bouchon, a Michelin-starred restaurant renowned for its impeccable service and exquisite dishes. Their menu showcases the finest seasonal ingredients, transformed into masterpieces of flavor and presentation. For a taste of coastal elegance, head to The Lark, a vibrant restaurant in the Funk Zone, where the menu features fresh, locally sourced seafood and produce.

Price Range:

Bouchon: $75-$120 per person

The Lark: $50-$80 per person

A Culinary Journey Beyond Expectations

Santa Barbara's farm-to-table scene is a testament to the region's deep connection to its agricultural roots. With its unwavering commitment to freshness, sustainability, and culinary excellence, Santa Barbara offers a culinary journey beyond expectations, delighting every palate with a symphony of flavors that celebrate the bounty of the land and sea.

9.3 Popular Restaurants

Santa Barbara boasts a vibrant culinary scene, offering a diverse array of flavors to tantalize every palate. From fresh seafood to mouthwatering Mexican fare, the city's restaurants showcase the region's rich culinary heritage and innovative culinary creativity. Here's a glimpse into some of Santa Barbara's most popular restaurants, along with their opening and closing hours:

The Black Sheep: This stylish and cozy gastropub presents a delightful fusion of French and Asian-inspired

American cuisine. Their menu features delectable dishes like the 48-hour braised beef short ribs with parsnip puree and vegetables, and the pan-seared scallops with cauliflower puree, crispy prosciutto, and caper brown butter. **Open from 5:00 PM to 10:00 PM on Fridays and Saturdays, and 5:00 PM to 9:00 PM on Tuesdays, Wednesdays, Sundays, and Thursdays.**

Finch & Fork: This charming New American restaurant embodies the essence of Santa Barbara's farm-to-table philosophy. Their menu showcases locally sourced ingredients, transformed into culinary masterpieces like the roasted cauliflower steak with tahini dressing, pomegranate molasses, and candied almonds, or the grilled octopus with smoked paprika aioli, roasted fingerlings, and chorizo. **Open for breakfast, brunch, and dinner, Finch & Fork is open from 7:00 AM to 9:00 PM daily.**

Boathouse at Hendry's Beach: Perched on the sandy shores of Hendry's Beach, this upscale seafood restaurant offers breathtaking ocean views alongside exquisite culinary delights. Their menu features fresh seafood delicacies like the grilled branzino with roasted fennel, blood orange, and caper beurre blanc, or the pan-seared scallops with butternut squash puree, Brussels sprouts, and brown butter sage. **Open from 7:30 AM to 9:00**

PM daily, the Boathouse exudes a relaxed coastal ambiance.

Bettina: Nestled in the charming town of Montecito, Bettina is a haven for pizza lovers. Their wood-fired pizzas are crafted with fresh, high-quality ingredients, resulting in perfectly charred crusts and tantalizing toppings. Try their signature Bettina pizza, topped with mozzarella, caramelized onions, pancetta, and black pepper, or the vegetarian delight, the Ortolana, featuring grilled zucchini, eggplant, red bell peppers, and basil. **Open for lunch and dinner, Bettina is open from 11:30 AM to 9:00 PM daily.**

Sama Sama Kitchen: This vibrant Asian fusion restaurant embraces the flavors of Southeast Asia, offering a culinary journey through Thailand, Vietnam, and Indonesia. Their menu features authentic dishes like the Thai green curry with chicken, bamboo shoots, and Thai basil, or the Vietnamese pho with rice noodles, beef brisket, and fresh herbs. **Open for lunch and dinner, Sama Sama Kitchen is open from 11:00 AM to 10:00 PM daily.**

These are just a few of the many exceptional restaurants that Santa Barbara has to offer. Whether you're craving fresh seafood, mouthwatering Mexican fare, or innovative Asian fusion, Santa Barbara's culinary scene promises an unforgettable dining experience.

9.4 Farmers' Markets

Santa Barbara is renowned for its vibrant farmers' markets, where visitors and locals alike can indulge in the bounty of fresh, locally grown produce, artisanal goods, and delectable prepared foods. These markets, scattered throughout the city, offer a delightful immersion into the region's rich agricultural heritage and culinary creativity. **Here's a glimpse into some of Santa Barbara's most popular farmers' markets, along with their opening and closing hours:**

Downtown Santa Barbara Farmers Market: Held every Saturday morning from 8:00 AM to 1:00 PM on Santa Barbara and Cota Streets, this bustling market showcases a wide array of fresh produce, from vibrant fruits and vegetables to fragrant herbs and colorful flowers. Strolling through the market, you'll encounter a diverse selection of vendors offering everything from sun-ripened tomatoes to plump berries, crisp lettuces, and freshly dug root vegetables.

Goleta Farmers Market: Nestled in the heart of Goleta, this weekly market takes place every Sunday from 10:00 AM to 2:00 PM at the Fairview Shopping Center. Here, you'll discover a delightful array of locally grown produce, alongside artisanal crafts, baked goods, and prepared foods. Sample fresh-baked bread, indulge in homemade jams and preserves, or savor a delicious lunch from one of the market's food vendors.

Old Town Santa Barbara Farmers Market: Immerse yourself in the charm of Old Town Santa Barbara at this lively farmers market, **held every Tuesday from 3:00 PM to 6:30 PM** on Anacapa Street between Figueroa and Chapala Streets. This market features a vibrant selection of locally grown produce, along with handcrafted goods, artisanal treats, and prepared foods. Enjoy the vibrant atmosphere, mingle with local artisans, and discover the unique flavors of Santa Barbara's culinary scene.

Solvang Farmers Market: Experience the Danish charm of Solvang at this weekly farmers market, **held every Thursday from 3:00 PM to 6:00 PM on Mission Drive near the Solvang Festival Theater.** This market offers a delightful selection of fresh produce, alongside Danish pastries, artisanal crafts, and prepared foods. Enjoy the lively atmosphere, savor authentic Danish pastries, and discover the unique flavors of Solvang's culinary heritage.

Carpinteria Farmers Market: Nestled in the charming coastal town of Carpinteria, **this weekly market takes place every Wednesday from 3:00 PM to 6:30 PM at the Carpinteria Community Farmers Market.** Here, you'll discover a bountiful selection of fresh produce, alongside artisanal crafts, baked goods, and prepared foods. Enjoy the laid-back atmosphere, sample local delicacies, and savor the flavors of Carpinteria's agricultural bounty.

These farmers' markets not only provide access to fresh, locally grown produce but also offer a vibrant glimpse into Santa Barbara's diverse culinary traditions and the passion of its local farmers and artisans. Whether seeking seasonal produce, handcrafted goods, or delectable treats, Santa Barbara's farmers' markets promise an unforgettable experience.

NOTE

_____

_____

_____

_____

_____

CHAPTER TEN

Shopping

10.1 Unique Boutiques

Santa Barbara, nestled along the scenic California coastline, is a haven for unique boutiques offering an eclectic mix of fashion, home décor, and handcrafted treasures. These charming shops provide a delightful respite from the bustling crowds, allowing visitors to immerse themselves in the town's vibrant and creative spirit.

Here are a few of Santa Barbara's most captivating boutiques, each with its own distinct personality and allure:

Lovebird Boutique & Jewelry Bar: Located at 7 E De La Guerra St, this charming boutique exudes a warm and inviting ambiance, showcasing a curated collection of women's apparel and accessories. From breezy dresses and stylish tops to delicate jewelry and eye-catching handbags, Lovebird caters to the discerning fashion-conscious individual. **Opening Hours: Tuesday-Sunday 11am-5:30pm**

The Blue Door: Nestled within the historic La Arcada shopping complex, The Blue Door beckons with its vibrant bohemian spirit. This eclectic boutique brims with an artful assortment of clothing, jewelry, home décor, and handcrafted gifts, each piece infused with a touch of whimsy and global inspiration. **Opening Hours: Monday-Saturday 11am-6pm, Sunday 12pm-5pm**

The Shopkeepers: Situated on the bustling State Street, The Shopkeepers is a treasure trove of locally sourced and curated goods. This vibrant shop features an ever-changing selection of women's and men's apparel, accessories, home décor, and artisan-crafted items, all reflecting the unique character of Santa Barbara. **Opening Hours: Monday-Saturday 10am-6pm, Sunday 11am-5pm**

Diani Living: Indulge in the art of home décor at Diani Living, a haven for those seeking to elevate their living spaces. This stylish boutique on State Street presents an exquisite collection of furnishings, accessories, and home accents, all carefully selected for their quality, craftsmanship, and timeless appeal. **Opening Hours: Monday-Saturday 10am-6pm, Sunday 11am-5pm**

Jake & Jones: Elevate your wardrobe with a touch of refined elegance at Jake & Jones, a boutique specializing in men's apparel and accessories. This sophisticated shop on State Street curates a collection of classic and contemporary clothing, footwear, and accessories, catering to the discerning gentleman. **Opening Hours: Monday-Saturday 10am-6pm, Sunday 11am-5pm**

Loveworn: Located in the heart of the Funk Zone, Loveworn embodies the eclectic spirit of this vibrant neighborhood. This vintage boutique offers a treasure trove of pre-loved clothing, jewelry, and accessories, each piece carefully selected for its unique style and timeless appeal. **Opening Hours: Tuesday-Sunday 11am-5pm**

Ace Rivington: Discover the intersection of fashion and art at Ace Rivington, a contemporary boutique on State Street. This forward-thinking shop showcases a curated collection of men's and women's apparel, accessories, and home décor, all inspired by a blend of modern and vintage aesthetics. **Opening Hours: Monday-Saturday 11am-6pm, Sunday 11am-5pm**

Catherine Gee: Immerse yourself in the world of fine jewelry at Catherine Gee, a boutique on State Street renowned for its exquisite craftsmanship and impeccable design. This elegant shop presents a collection of handcrafted jewelry pieces, each showcasing the artistry

and passion of its creators. **Opening Hours: Monday-Saturday 10am-6pm, Sunday 11am-5pm**
As you stroll through the charming streets of Santa Barbara, be sure to venture into these unique boutiques, where you'll discover hidden gems and treasures that reflect the town's rich heritage and creative spirit.

10.2 Santa Barbara Souvenirs

Nestled along the picturesque Californian coast, Santa Barbara exudes an enchanting blend of Spanish colonial heritage, vibrant art scene, and idyllic beaches. To capture the essence of this captivating city, visitors seek out souvenirs that reflect its unique character and serve as a lasting reminder of their time spent in this coastal paradise.

Culinary Delights from Santa Barbara's Bounty

Santa Barbara's fertile coastal landscape and rich culinary traditions give rise to a delectable array of souvenirs to tantalize the taste buds. Sample locally produced wines from esteemed vineyards, savor the sweetness of fresh-picked strawberries, or indulge in a jar of honey infused with the delicate aroma of coastal lavender. A selection of artisanal cheeses, olive oils, and gourmet sea salts will transport you back to the sun-kissed hills and briny shores of Santa Barbara.

Artistic Expressions of Santa Barbara's Creative Spirit

Santa Barbara is a haven for artists and artisans, and their vibrant creations make for cherished souvenirs. Handcrafted jewelry adorned with semiprecious stones mined from local mountains captures the city's natural beauty. Hand-painted ceramics showcase the region's artistic heritage, while locally woven textiles and handcrafted baskets reflect the rich cultural tapestry of Santa Barbara.

Beach Treasures from Santa Barbara's Coastal Playground

Santa Barbara's beaches are a haven for sun-seekers and nature enthusiasts alike. A collection of seashells, each with its unique shape and pattern, serves as a reminder of leisurely strolls along the sandy shores. A hand-painted surfboard, adorned with vibrant surfers and crashing waves, embodies the city's surfing culture. A weathered piece of driftwood, transformed into a decorative accent, brings a touch of coastal charm to any home.

Commemorative Keepsakes of Santa Barbara's Landmarks

Santa Barbara's architectural gems and historical landmarks provide inspiration for memorable souvenirs. A miniature replica of the iconic Mission Santa Barbara, with its red-tiled roof and graceful arches, captures the city's Spanish heritage. A postcard featuring the majestic Courthouse Tower, a symbol of Santa Barbara's architectural elegance, serves as a picturesque reminder of the city's skyline.

Apparel and Accessories Infused with Santa Barbara's Style

Santa Barbara's laid-back coastal vibe translates into stylish souvenirs that reflect the city's relaxed yet refined aesthetic. A pair of sunglasses with the city's name etched on the temples adds a touch of Santa Barbara flair to any outfit. A t-shirt adorned with a whimsical illustration of a sea lion or a palm tree captures the city's playful spirit. A locally designed beach towel, featuring vibrant stripes inspired by the sunsets over the Pacific, brings a touch of Santa Barbara's beachside charm to any pool or patio.

10.3 Shopping Districts

Santa Barbara offers a diverse range of shopping districts, each with its own unique charm and character.

Here are a few of the most popular districts:

Paseo Nuevo: This open-air mall is located in the heart of downtown Santa Barbara and features a variety of well-known chain retailers, plus a movie theater and dining options. **It is open from 11:00 AM to 7:00 PM Monday through Saturday and 11:00 AM to 6:00 PM on Sunday.**

La Arcada Plaza: This quaint shopping and dining district is located in a beautifully landscaped plaza with Spanish Colonial Revival architecture. It is home to a variety of boutiques, art galleries, and restaurants. **It is open from 11:00 AM to 5:00 PM on Tuesday through Friday, 11:00 AM to 8:00 PM on Thursday, and 11:00 AM to 5:00 PM on Saturday and Sunday.**

Santa Barbara Plaza: This outdoor shopping center is located just off of State Street and features a variety of national retailers, as well as local shops and restaurants. **It is open from 10:00 AM to 9:00 PM Monday through Friday, 10:00 AM to 8:00 PM on Saturday, and 11:00 AM to 6:00 PM on Sunday.**

Arlington Plaza: This neighborhood shopping center is located in the Arlington Heights neighborhood and features a variety of local shops and restaurants. **It is open from 9:30 AM to 8:30 PM Monday through Saturday and 10:00 AM to 7:00 PM on Sunday.**

Milpas Shopping Center: This neighborhood shopping center is located in the Milpas Street neighborhood and features a variety of grocery stores, drugstores, and other essential businesses. **It is open from 6:00 AM to 11:00 PM Monday through Friday, 6:00 AM to 12:00 AM on Saturday, and 6:00 AM to 11:00 PM on Sunday.**

These are just a few of the many great shopping districts in Santa Barbara. With so many options to choose from, you're sure to find the perfect place to shop, dine, and explore.

CHAPTER ELEVEN

Nightlife

11.1 Bars And Pubs

Santa Barbara, California is a coastal town known for its stunning beaches, beautiful architecture, and vibrant arts scene. But beyond its picturesque attractions, Santa Barbara also boasts a thriving nightlife, with a wide variety of bars and pubs to cater to every taste and preference.

For the Pub Purists:

Old Kings Road: Located in the heart of downtown Santa Barbara, Old Kings Road is a classic British-style pub, complete with dark wood paneling, cozy booths, and a fireplace. The menu features an extensive selection of beers, both domestic and imported, as well as traditional pub fare like fish and chips and bangers and mash.

Dargan's Irish Pub: For a taste of Ireland, head to Dargan's Irish Pub, where the Guinness flows freely and the live music fills the air. This lively pub is a popular spot for locals and tourists alike, and it's a great place to catch a game of rugby or just enjoy a pint with friends.

The Good Lion: If you're looking for a more upscale pub experience, The Good Lion is the place to go. This polished gastropub offers a menu of elevated British classics, such as braised short ribs and roasted bone marrow. The bar also boasts an impressive selection of whiskies and scotches.

For the Cocktail Enthusiasts:

O'Malleys Bar: O'Malleys Bar is a sophisticated cocktail bar with a vintage Hollywood vibe. The knowledgeable bartenders can whip up any of your favorite classic cocktails, or you can try one of their signature concoctions. The bar also has a small but well-curated selection of wines and beers.

Shaker Mill: Shaker Mill is a hidden gem in the Funk Zone, a hip neighborhood known for its art galleries, boutiques, and trendy restaurants. This cozy cocktail bar specializes in craft cocktails made with fresh, seasonal ingredients. The bar also has a small patio, perfect for people-watching.

Lama Dog Tap Room + Bottle Shop: For a taste of local craft beer, head to Lama Dog Tap Room + Bottle Shop. This friendly neighborhood bar has a rotating selection of beers on tap, as well as a wide variety of bottled beers to take home. The bar also hosts regular events, such as live music nights and trivia nights.

For the Night Owls:

Satellite: Satellite is a popular late-night spot in the Funk Zone, with a lively atmosphere and a diverse crowd. The bar has a large dance floor and a DJ spinning tunes until the early hours of the morning.

Crocodile Restaurant and Bar at the Lemon Tree Inn: For a more upscale late-night experience, head to Crocodile Restaurant and Bar at the Lemon Tree Inn. This sophisticated bar has a relaxed atmosphere and a menu of light bites, perfect for late-night snacking. The bar also has a live music program, with jazz and blues bands performing on weekends.

Speakeasy at Plow & Angel: If you're looking for a unique late-night experience, check out the Speakeasy at Plow & Angel. This hidden bar is accessible through a secret door in the restaurant, and it features a vintage atmosphere and a menu of craft cocktails.

11.2 Live Music Venues

Nestled along the sun-kissed shores of California's Central Coast, Santa Barbara is a haven for music lovers, boasting an eclectic array of live music venues that cater to every taste and genre. From intimate listening rooms to open-air amphitheaters, Santa Barbara's music scene pulsates with energy and creativity, offering a harmonious blend of established acts and up-and-coming talents.

Santa Barbara Bowl: A crown jewel of Santa Barbara's entertainment scene, the Santa Barbara Bowl is an iconic outdoor amphitheater nestled amidst the picturesque foothills of the Santa Ynez Mountains. Since its inception in 1936, the Bowl has hosted legendary performers from every musical genre, from rock and pop icons to jazz legends and classical orchestras. Its stunning natural setting, state-of-the-art sound system, and spacious lawn seating make it a truly enchanting venue.

Granada Theatre: For a taste of elegance and grandeur, the Granada Theatre is a must-visit destination. This opulent Spanish Colonial Revival-style theater, built in 1924, has hosted a diverse array of performances, from Broadway shows and ballet recitals to symphony orchestras and jazz ensembles. Its ornate interior, impeccable acoustics, and rich history make it a cherished landmark in Santa Barbara's arts scene.

SOhO Restaurant & Music Club: In the heart of downtown Santa Barbara, SOhO Restaurant & Music Club offers an intimate and vibrant setting for live music. This eclectic venue showcases a diverse range of genres, from indie rock and folk to soul and funk. Its warm and inviting atmosphere, coupled with its commitment to up-and-coming artists, has earned it a reputation as a beloved local haunt.

Lobero Theatre: Steeped in history and tradition, the Lobero Theatre is a stunning example of Neo-Romanesque architecture. Built in 1873, the theater has hosted a diverse array of performers, from vaudeville acts and silent films to classical music concerts and contemporary dance performances. Its intimate setting, rich acoustics, and elegant ambiance make it a cherished venue for both locals and visitors.

UCSB Arts & Lectures: The University of California, Santa Barbara's Arts & Lectures program brings world-renowned performers to the campus, offering a diverse range of cultural experiences. From classical music concerts and Broadway shows to lectures by renowned authors and scientists, the program provides a vibrant intellectual and artistic tapestry for the community.

Beyond the Main Stage:

Santa Barbara's live music scene extends beyond its iconic venues, with numerous smaller bars, clubs, and restaurants hosting a variety of musical performances. From blues and jazz nights at local watering holes to folk and acoustic sets in cozy cafes, Santa Barbara's intimate music scene offers a wealth of hidden gems waiting to be discovered.

Whether you're seeking the thrill of a sold-out concert at the Santa Barbara Bowl or the intimate charm of a local music club, Santa Barbara's live music scene offers an unforgettable experience for every music lover.

11.3 Entertainment Options

Nestled along the picturesque Californian coast, Santa Barbara is a haven for entertainment enthusiasts, offering a diverse array of activities and attractions to suit every taste and preference. Whether you're seeking cultural immersion, outdoor adventures, or family-friendly fun, Santa Barbara has something to captivate your senses and create lasting memories.

Immerse Yourself in Art and Culture

For art aficionados, Santa Barbara boasts a vibrant arts scene that spans museums, galleries, and performing arts venues. The Santa Barbara Museum of Art, with its extensive collection of American and European paintings, is a must-visit for art lovers. The Santa Barbara Botanic Garden, awash with diverse flora, provides a tranquil escape into nature's artistry. For those seeking theatrical delights, the Granada Theatre, with its opulent architecture and captivating performances, offers an unforgettable experience.

Indulge in Outdoor Adventures

Santa Barbara's stunning natural beauty provides the perfect backdrop for outdoor enthusiasts. Hike amidst breathtaking coastal landscapes, kayak along the pristine waters of the Pacific Ocean, or surf the waves that roll onto the sandy shores. For a truly unique experience, embark on a whale-watching excursion to witness these majestic marine giants in their natural habitat.

Explore the Funk Zone

Immerse yourself in the vibrant ambiance of the Funk Zone, a hub for artisan food producers, craft breweries, and eclectic boutiques. Indulge in culinary delights at the Public Market, savor craft brews at one of the local breweries, or discover unique treasures at the eclectic shops that line the streets.

Family-Friendly Entertainment

Santa Barbara caters to families with a variety of kid-friendly attractions. MOXI, The Wolf Museum of Exploration + Innovation, sparks curiosity and imagination with its interactive exhibits. The Santa Barbara Zoo, home to a diverse range of animals, provides educational and entertaining encounters with the animal kingdom. For a splash of fun, visit the Santa Barbara Water Park, where water slides, lazy rivers, and a wave pool await.

Evening Delights

As the sun sets, Santa Barbara's nightlife comes alive with a variety of entertainment options. Catch a live music performance at one of the city's renowned venues, such as The Arlington Theatre or The Lobero Theatre. Enjoy a romantic dinner at one of the many fine dining restaurants, or dance the night away at one of the lively clubs.

With its diverse cultural offerings, stunning natural beauty, and family-friendly attractions, Santa Barbara is an entertainment paradise, inviting visitors to explore, discover, and create unforgettable memories.

CHAPTER TWELVE

Day Trips From Santa Barbara

12.1 Wine Country

Getting There:

The drive from Santa Barbara to Wine Country is approximately 423 miles and takes about 6 hours and 45 minutes. The most direct route is to take US-101 N. You can also take a more scenic route along the coast, but this will add some time to your trip.

Entry Fee:

There is no general entry fee for Wine Country. However, some wineries may charge a tasting fee, which typically ranges from $20 to $50 per person.

Things to Do:

Visit Wineries: There are over 400 wineries in Wine Country, so you'll have plenty of options to choose from. Some of the most popular wineries include:

Napa Valley: V. Sattui Winery, Castello di Amorosa, Sterling Vineyards, Francis Ford Coppola Winery

Sonoma Valley: Kunde Family Winery, Ravenswood Winery, Ferrari-Carano Winery, J.J. Prüm Winery

Explore the Outdoors: Wine Country is a beautiful place to enjoy the outdoors. There are many hiking trails, biking trails, and parks to explore. Some of the most popular outdoor activities include:

Hiking: Hike to the top of Mount St. Helena for stunning views of the valley.

Biking: Rent a bike and ride along the Napa Valley Vine Trail.

Picnic: Enjoy a picnic lunch at one of the many parks in Wine Country.

Enjoy the Arts and Culture: Wine Country is home to a number of art galleries, museums, and theaters. Some of the most popular arts and culture attractions include:

Art Galleries: The Hess Collection, di Rosa Center for Contemporary Art, Napa Valley Museum

Museums: Charles M. Schulz Museum, Walt Disney Family Museum, Sonoma Valley Museum of Art

Theaters: Napa Valley Opera House, Sonoma County Repertory Theater, Transcendence Theatre Company

Dine at Michelin-Starred Restaurants: Wine Country is home to a number of Michelin-starred restaurants. Some of the most popular Michelin-starred restaurants include:

Napa Valley: The French Laundry, Restaurant at Meadowood, The Farmhouse at Carneros

Sonoma Valley: SingleThread, Sushi Ran, La Toque

Tips:

Book your winery tastings in advance: Wineries can get crowded, especially on weekends. It's a good idea to book your tastings in advance to avoid disappointment.

Pack comfortable shoes: You'll be doing a lot of walking, so be sure to pack comfortable shoes.

Bring a hat and sunscreen: The weather in Wine Country can be warm and sunny, so be sure to bring a hat and sunscreen.

Don't forget to drink water: It's important to stay hydrated, especially if you're drinking wine.

Have fun!: Wine Country is a beautiful place to relax and enjoy the good things in life. So take your time, savor the wine, and enjoy the scenery.

12.2 Solvang

Solvang, a Danish town nestled in the Santa Ynez Valley, is a charming destination for a day trip from Santa Barbara. The town is known for its Danish architecture, bakeries, and wineries.

How to Get There

The drive from Santa Barbara to Solvang is approximately 35 miles and takes about 50 minutes. You can take either Highway 154 or Highway 246.

Entry Fee

Most of the attractions in Solvang are free to visit. However, there are a few places that charge an entry fee, such as:

- Mission San Miguel Arcángel: $5 for adults, $3 for children ages 6-12, and free for children under 5.

- Hans Christian Andersen Museum: $5 for adults, $3 for children ages 6-12, and free for children under 5.

- Solvang Festival Theater: Ticket prices vary depending on the performance.

Things to Do

Explore the Danish architecture: Stroll down the streets of Solvang and admire the Danish-style buildings.

Visit the Mission San Miguel Arcángel: This Franciscan mission was founded in 1787 and is one of the most beautiful missions in California.

Sample Danish pastries: Solvang is home to many bakeries that sell traditional Danish pastries, such as kringle and æbleskiver.

Go wine tasting: Solvang is located in the heart of Santa Ynez Valley, which is known for its wineries. There are many wineries in Solvang that offer wine tasting.

Attend a festival: Solvang hosts a number of festivals throughout the year, such as Danish Days and Julefest.

Here is a suggested itinerary for a day trip from Santa Barbara to Solvang:

Morning:

Drive from Santa Barbara to Solvang (50 minutes)

Explore the Danish architecture

Visit the Mission San Miguel Arcángel

Afternoon:

Sample Danish pastries

Go wine tasting

Evening:

Attend a festival (if applicable)

Drive back to Santa Barbara

Tips

Start your day early: Solvang is a small town, so you can see most of the attractions in a day. However, if you want to take your time and enjoy the town, start your day early.

Pack a picnic lunch: There are many picnic spots in Solvang, so you can pack a lunch and enjoy a meal outdoors.

Wear comfortable shoes: You will be doing a lot of walking, so wear comfortable shoes.

Be prepared for crowds: Solvang is a popular tourist destination, so be prepared for crowds, especially during peak season.

12.3 Channel Islands National Park

Escape the bustling city and embark on an unforgettable day trip from Santa Barbara to the Channel Islands National Park, a captivating archipelago teeming with natural wonders and rich history. Immerse yourself in the park's diverse ecosystems, encounter its fascinating wildlife, and delve into its captivating past.

Getting There

The Channel Islands National Park is an archipelago of five islands off the coast of Southern California. The most accessible islands for day trips from Santa Barbara are Santa Cruz Island and Anacapa Island.

Island Packers Cruises: The official boat concessionaire for the Channel Islands National Park, Island Packers Cruises offers daily transportation to Santa Cruz Island and Anacapa Island from the Santa Barbara Harbor. Their boats are comfortable and well-equipped for the journey, and they offer a variety of tour options to suit different interests.

Entry Fee

The entrance fee for Channel Islands National Park is $15 for adults and $8 for children ages 16 and under. The fee is valid for seven days and can be purchased at the Island Packers Cruises office or online.

Things to Do

Hiking: Explore the diverse trails on Santa Cruz Island, ranging from easy strolls along the coast to challenging hikes to the summit of Cavern Point. Enjoy breathtaking views of the Pacific Ocean, spot unique island plants and wildlife, and discover remnants of human habitation dating back thousands of years.

Kayaking: Embark on a guided kayaking tour through the kelp forests and sea caves of Santa Cruz Island. Paddle alongside seals and sea lions, marvel at the colorful marine life, and experience the thrill of exploring hidden coves.

Snorkeling and Diving: Immerse yourself in the vibrant underwater world of the Channel Islands National Park. Snorkel or scuba dive among kelp forests, encounter a variety of fish species, and witness the mesmerizing beauty of coral reefs.

Wildlife Viewing: Keep your eyes peeled for the abundant wildlife that calls the Channel Islands home. Spot harbor seals lounging on the rocks, watch California sea lions frolicking in the water, and observe a variety of seabirds, including pelicans, cormorants, and gulls.

Island Interpretation: Learn about the natural and cultural history of the Channel Islands through guided walks, ranger talks, and exhibits at the Visitor Center on Santa Cruz Island. Discover the unique geology of the islands, their role as a refuge for endangered species, and the fascinating stories of the Chumash people who once inhabited the islands.

NOTE

CHAPTER THIRTEEN

Practical Information

13.1 Transportation Within Santa Barbara

Nestled along the picturesque California coastline, Santa Barbara offers visitors a captivating blend of urban charm and coastal beauty. Whether you're exploring the city's vibrant downtown, strolling along the sandy beaches, or venturing into the surrounding wine country, Santa Barbara's diverse transportation options ensure a seamless and enjoyable travel experience.

Public Transportation: Efficient and Affordable

Santa Barbara's Metropolitan Transit District (MTD) operates an extensive bus system that connects various neighborhoods, attractions, and surrounding communities. With a single fare starting at $1.75, MTD buses offer a convenient and affordable way to navigate the city. Frequent schedules and user-friendly online trip planning tools make commuting a breeze.

For those seeking a more scenic and leisurely journey, the Santa Barbara Trolley provides a delightful alternative. Hop on and off at designated stops along a charming route that winds through the city's historic landmarks and picturesque neighborhoods. Tickets range from $15 for adults and $7 for children.

Water Taxi: A Unique and Serene Experience

Experience Santa Barbara's breathtaking coastline from a unique perspective by taking a ride on the Santa Barbara Water Taxi. This charming shuttle service connects the harbor area, the Funk Zone, and the popular East Beach, offering stunning views of the city and the Pacific Ocean. One-way fares start at $6 for adults and $3 for children.

Biking: Eco-friendly Exploration

Santa Barbara's flat terrain and extensive network of bike paths make it an ideal destination for cyclists. Rent a bike from one of the many bike rental shops and explore the city at your own pace. Cruise along the Cabrillo Bike Path, which hugs the coastline, or pedal through the vibrant streets of downtown.

Taxi and Ride-Sharing Services: Convenient and Reliable

For those seeking a quick and convenient transportation option, taxi and ride-sharing services like Uber and Lyft are readily available in Santa Barbara. Fares vary depending on the distance traveled and time of day, but they typically start around $10-15 for a short trip.

Pedicabs: A Whimsical Ride

Add a touch of whimsy to your Santa Barbara adventure by taking a ride in one of the city's charming pedicabs. These pedal-powered rickshaws offer a unique way to explore the city's streets and soak up the sights and sounds. Fares typically start around $20-25 for a short trip.

Parking: A Breeze Compared to Major Cities

Parking in Santa Barbara is relatively affordable and convenient compared to major cities. Street parking is available in many areas, and hourly rates are typically between $1-2. Metered parking is enforced in certain areas, so be sure to check signage carefully. Several parking garages and lots are also available, offering a more secure option for longer stays.

Accessibility: Options for All

Santa Barbara is committed to providing accessible transportation options for all residents and visitors. MTD buses are equipped with ramps and designated seating areas for passengers with disabilities. Additionally, the city offers a paratransit service for individuals who are unable to use fixed-route buses.

With its diverse range of transportation options, Santa Barbara caters to every preference and need, making it a truly accessible and enjoyable city to explore. Whether you opt for the convenience of public transportation, the charm of a trolley ride, or the exhilaration of cycling along the coast, Santa Barbara ensures a smooth and memorable travel experience.

Tips for Getting Around Santa Barbara

- If you're planning on using public transportation, be sure to check the MTD website for schedules and route maps.

- If you're using a ridesharing service, be sure to have the app downloaded and your payment information on file before you request a ride.

- If you're taking a taxi, be sure to ask for an estimate of the fare before you get in the car.

- If you're biking, be sure to wear a helmet and follow the rules of the road.

- If you're walking, be sure to be aware of your surroundings and wear comfortable shoes.

13.2 Safety Tips

Santa Barbara is a welcoming and safe community, but like any city, it's important to be aware of your surroundings and take precautions to protect yourself.

General Safety Tips

Be aware of your surroundings: Pay attention to your surroundings and avoid distractions like your phone. Trust your instincts and if something doesn't feel right, remove yourself from the situation.

Stay in well-lit areas: Avoid walking alone in dark or secluded areas at night. If you must walk alone, stick to well-lit streets and consider using a personal alarm or carrying a flashlight.

Be cautious with valuables: Keep your valuables out of sight and avoid carrying large amounts of cash. If you're using a backpack, keep it close to you and zipped up.

Be mindful of alcohol consumption: Excessive alcohol consumption can impair your judgment and make you more vulnerable to crime. Drink responsibly and have a designated driver or arrange for a safe ride home.

Report suspicious activity: If you see something suspicious, don't hesitate to report it to law enforcement. Call 911 for emergencies or the Santa Barbara Police Department's non-emergency line at (805) 967-4488.

Safety Tips for Specific Activities

Beaches: Be aware of rip currents and swim only in designated areas. Follow lifeguard instructions and don't swim under the influence of alcohol.

Hiking and Trails: Stay on designated trails and avoid hiking alone. Let someone know where you're going and when you expect to return. Carry a map, compass, and plenty of water.

Downtown and Tourist Areas: Be cautious with your belongings and avoid carrying large purses or backpacks. Keep an eye on your children and avoid letting them wander off.

Nightlife: If you're going out at night, stick to well-lit and populated areas. Let someone know where you're going and when you expect to return. Use a designated ride-sharing service or a trusted taxi company.

By following these safety tips, you can minimize your risk of becoming a victim of crime and enjoy your time in Santa Barbara safely.

13.3 Local Custom And Etiquette

Santa Barbara, a charming coastal town nestled along the California Riviera, is known for its laid-back atmosphere, friendly locals, and rich cultural heritage. While the town embraces a casual and relaxed vibe, there are certain customs and etiquette norms that are valued by the community.

Greetings and Friendliness: Santa Barbara is known for its welcoming spirit. A simple "hello" or a nod with a smile is a common way to acknowledge others, whether it's a fellow shopper, a dog walker, or someone you meet on the street.

Respecting the Environment: Santa Barbara takes pride in its natural beauty and environmental consciousness. Be mindful of littering, conserve water, and respect public spaces like beaches and parks.

Outdoor Etiquette: Santa Barbara's beaches, hiking trails, and parks are cherished recreational spaces. Be considerate of fellow users, keep noise levels low, and dispose of trash properly.

Dining Etiquette: Santa Barbara offers a diverse culinary scene, from casual cafes to fine-dining establishments. In casual settings, tipping 15-20% is customary. For fine dining, 20% is standard, and you may encounter a dress code.

Respecting Local Traditions: Santa Barbara celebrates its rich cultural heritage through various events and festivals. Be respectful of local customs and traditions during these occasions.

Community Involvement: Santa Barbara is a community-oriented town. Consider participating in local events, volunteering your time, or supporting local businesses.

Appreciating the Slow Pace: Santa Barbara embraces a slower pace of life. Relax, take your time, and savor the town's charm without rushing through experiences.

Respecting Local Diversity: Santa Barbara is a diverse community. Be respectful of different cultures, backgrounds, and beliefs.

Being a Responsible Visitor: Santa Barbara welcomes visitors, but be a responsible guest. Follow local rules, respect private property, and leave no trace of your presence.

Expressing Gratitude: A simple "thank you" goes a long way in Santa Barbara. Express gratitude to those who help you, whether it's a server, a shopkeeper, or a fellow traveler.

13.4 Emergency Number

In case of an emergency while visiting Santa Barbara, it's crucial to know the appropriate contact information for assistance.

Life-threatening Emergencies:

Call 911: For any life-threatening emergency, such as a fire, medical emergency, or crime in progress, dial 911 immediately.

Non-Emergency Matters:

Santa Barbara Police Department: For non-emergency police assistance, call (805) 882-8900.

Santa Barbara County Fire Department: For non-emergency fire or medical assistance, call (805) 683-3711.

Additional Resources:

Santa Barbara Cottage Hospital: For non-emergency medical assistance, visit Santa Barbara Cottage Hospital at 400 W Pueblo St, Santa Barbara, CA 93101 or call (805) 682-7111.

Santa Barbara County Sheriff's Office: For non-emergency law enforcement assistance in unincorporated areas of Santa Barbara County, call (805) 683-2724.

CHAPTER FOURTEEN

Conclusion

14.1 Final Thought

Santa Barbara, nestled along the picturesque California coastline, is a destination that effortlessly weaves together natural beauty, cultural richness, and a laid-back charm. As we conclude our journey through this captivating city in this travel guide, our final thoughts encapsulate the essence of Santa Barbara, offering readers a glimpse into the diverse tapestry that defines this coastal gem.

The heart of Santa Barbara beats to the rhythm of its stunning beaches, and our exploration begins with the golden shores that stretch along the Pacific Ocean. The sun-drenched sands of East Beach, framed by the iconic Stearns Wharf, invite visitors to bask in the warmth of the California sun or embark on a leisurely stroll along the palm-lined promenade. As the guide concludes, we reflect on the serene beauty of Butterfly Beach, where the sunset transforms the horizon into a canvas of vibrant hues, providing an idyllic end to a day of exploration.

Venturing beyond the beaches, the historic charm of Santa Barbara's architecture captures the imagination.

The distinctive red-tiled roofs and white-washed adobe facades of Spanish Colonial Revival buildings create a unique visual identity for the city. Our final thoughts highlight the architectural gems such as the Santa Barbara Courthouse and the Old Mission, each narrating a story of the city's rich history and cultural heritage. The guide encourages readers to wander through the red-bricked streets of downtown, where boutique shops, art galleries, and sidewalk cafes beckon, offering a blend of contemporary flair and timeless elegance.

A key aspect of Santa Barbara's allure lies in its commitment to preserving nature and fostering sustainability. The guide emphasizes the importance of exploring the Botanic Garden, where native flora thrives in a carefully curated environment, and the Santa Barbara Zoo, known for its conservation efforts and engaging exhibits. Our final thoughts applaud the city's dedication to environmental consciousness, encouraging travelers to appreciate and contribute to the preservation of the region's natural splendor.

The culinary scene in Santa Barbara is a celebration of flavors, and the guide leaves readers with a taste of the diverse gastronomic offerings. From fresh seafood at the harbor-side eateries to farm-to-table experiences in the Funk Zone, Santa Barbara's culinary landscape reflects the abundance of locally sourced ingredients. As readers savor their final thoughts, they are encouraged to indulge in the city's wine culture, exploring the vineyards of the Santa Ynez Valley, known for its world-class wineries and picturesque landscapes.

The people of Santa Barbara, known for their warmth and hospitality, form an integral part of the city's identity. The guide wraps up by highlighting the welcoming community spirit that permeates the city, fostering a sense of belonging for both residents and visitors. Whether engaging in a local festival, attending an outdoor concert, or simply enjoying a casual conversation with a fellow beachgoer, the social fabric of Santa Barbara adds an intangible, yet unforgettable, dimension to the travel experience.

In conclusion, this Santa Barbara travel guide aims to be more than just a compendium of tourist attractions; it aspires to be a companion that captures the spirit of a city that seamlessly blends nature, culture, and community. As readers close the guide, the hope is that the final thoughts linger—a melange of sunsets over the Pacific, the echoes of history in the architecture, the flavors of local cuisine, and the warmth of a community that invites all to share in the magic of Santa Barbara.

NOTE

_____

_____

_____

_____

_____

_____

_____

_____

_____

_____

_____

SAFE TRAVEL!

Made in the USA
Las Vegas, NV
14 January 2024

84323126R00085